THE • SKILLS • OF • THE • GAME

NETBALL

Betty Galsworthy

First Published in 1990 by
The Crowood Press Ltd
Ramsbury, Marlborough
Wiltshire SN8 2HR

www.crowood.com

Revised edition 1996

This impression 2005

British Library Cataloguing-in-Publication Data

A catalogue record for this book is available from the British Library

ISBN 1 86126 004 0

Acknowledgements
Thanks to the following for the action photograph:
Brian Worrell, All England Netball Association, Figs 30, 72, 107, 108, 113, 122, 138, 142, 169.
Bill Hickley, Figs 40 and 89.
Eileen Langsley, Figs 57, 106, 112, 177, 179.
Patsy Rochester, Figs 181, 184, 186, 187, 188.
Demonstration photographs by Brian Starbuck.
Author photograph courtesy of *Coventry Evening Telegraph*.
Cover photographs courtesy of Eileen Langsley.
Thanks to Paul Chokran for his advice on graphics and to Kim Pinney, Gill Davies, Liz Hawley
and Veronica Kavanagh for giving their time during the taking of the demonstration
photographs.

Line drawings by Jan Sparrow.

Typefaces used: text, Univers 55; headings, Univers 65 and Plantin.

Typeset and designed by
D & N Publishing
Membury Business Park, Lambourn Woodlands
Hungerford, Berkshire.

Printed by CPI Bath

Contents

In this newly revised edition Betty Galsworthy, one of England's most respected coaches, clearly explains these principles and provides a comprehensive guide to skills and techniques and how they can be applied tactically in the game.

Betty has worked very closely with the All England Netball Association to help raise the standards of coaches and coaching, and her accumulated learning and depth of experience both as a coach and umpire have established her as an acknowledged expert in the field. Drawing on a sound knowledge of all aspects of the game Betty provides information and ideas that will ensure coaches and players have a greater understanding of the many factors required for successful performance. Every chapter is well illustrated and easy to follow and is essential for all those wishing to improve their game.

Pauline Harrison
National Director of Coaching, AENA

Having known and been coached by Betty Galsworthy for more years than either of us care to remember, I felt very honoured when she asked me to review her book. When I read the title, *Netball, The Skills of the Game*, my immediate thoughts were 'Oh, not another book on netball', but read on – it is much more than that.

Whether young or old, experienced or a beginner, player or coach, there is something for everyone to read, learn and enjoy. As always, Betty has managed cunningly to combine the fitness angle into the practices and skills of the game to make the more tedious side of netball more enjoyable. The book contains lots of original ideas for stimulating players into action, as well as being instructive but interesting. I felt fitter just by reading it.

Gill Davies
Warwickshire County Coach and former
Vice-Captain of England

Betty Galsworthy has been involved in the sport of netball for thirty years, in roles as diverse as player, coach, umpire and selector for England. She is an Advanced Coach for the All England Netball Association (AENA) and has coached at all levels right up to the England National Squad. Her achievements include playing for England for three years, coaching the England under-21 team to second place in the 1988 Bicentennial Tournament in Australia and the England senior squad to fourth place in the World Championships of 1991, and being voted one of the British Association of National Coaches/Dextrosol Coaches of 1988.

A retired lecturer in physical education and a former school teacher, Betty has been involved in the production of the AENA's coaching videos and regularly contributes to its quarterly magazine, *Netball*.

The game of netball is skilful, fast-moving and dynamic, and requires players to make rapid decisions under constantly changing conditions. The fundamental principles of movement and ball skills can be applied at all levels of the game.

The interaction of skills and fitness provide the base for all outstanding games players; thereafter, understanding team-work consolidates performance. Good coaches seek to develop these aspects in practice sessions. New coaches want help, experienced coaches want stimulation.

This text, identifying as it does the components of fitness, skill and team-work and giving advice about methods of practising, reflects the experience of the coach who has motivated all levels of player from schoolgirls to national squad. By following the advice and being guided by the progressions implied, coaches of any experience should find the help or stimulation to extend their knowledge and develop their coaching procedures.

Mary Thomas
Advanced Coach, Umpire and Administrator, AENA

Introduction

Netball is a throwing and catching game. Goals are scored when the ball passes through a ring suspended on a post, one at each end of the court. The original British game was introduced by an American while he was lecturing to physical training teachers. It was near the end of the nineteenth century and he taught the game as a form of indoor basketball, but with few rules, no court markings and goals being scored by shooting the ball into a wastepaper basket suspended on the walls at either end of a hall. Later, another American visitor developed this game to resemble more closely the type of basketball being played by women in America. This early beginning evolved into the netball of today – boundaries of play were introduced, the court was divided into thirds, goal rings were added, a larger ball was used and some of the rules from early basketball were retained.

As the trainee teachers went out into the schools they took this game with them and it proved to be very popular, particularly in the inner city schools where playground space was limited. The game quickly became established and the first set of published rules was introduced by the Ling Association, a group organized by some ex-physical training students. The game was enjoyed so much that when many girls left school they wanted to carry on playing. The first clubs were set up, many of them run by works and factories. The game spread and in 1926 a meeting of schools, clubs and other adult

Fig 1 Action at an inter-county tournament.

organizations formed the All England Women's Netball Association. This led to the formation of the County Associations and the annual inter-county tournament as we know them today.

After the Second World War, when netball resumed, it was run by the newly named All England Netball Association (AENA). Works and district leagues were set up throughout the country and the standard of play improved dramatically. Netball became international in 1949 when England, Scotland and Wales competed in a triangular fixture. By 1956 England was travelling to South Africa and a team from Australia was visiting England. As other countries became involved the difference in rules became a problem. The solution was the formation of the International Federation of Women's Basketball and Netball the same year (1956) – later called the International Federation of Netball Associations (FNA) – and the introduction of an international code of rules. This meant that all countries had to accept changes in their domestic rules, but from then onwards events world-wide could take place. In 1963 the first World Tournament was held in England and eleven countries competed, Australia becoming the first World Champions, with New Zealand second and England third.

Since 1963, the World Championships have been held every four years in different locations around the world and returned to Birmingham in England in July 1995. The number of competing countries has gradually increased with twenty seven countries taking part in 1995. The three major countries, England, Australia and New Zealand, have continued to dominate the top four places, but their dominance has been challenged by the threat from the strong netball-playing countries in the Caribbean. Trinidad and Tobago, and Jamaica have brought a different style and flair to the game with Trinidad sharing the title in 1979. South Africa returned to international competition in 1994 and came close to winning the 1995 championship, losing to Australia with New Zealand third and England again filling fourth position. The World Games, a competition held for non-Olympic Sports, was held in Europe in both 1989 and 1993 and hopefully will widen the spread of netball within the European Community. Netball was proud to be one of the new team sports to take part in the Commonwealth Games in Malaysia in 1998 where England competed strongly to win the Bronze Medal behind Australia and New Zealand.

Past presidents of the All England Netball Association have continually campaigned for the spread of the game: 'Netball must emerge from the school playground' demanded Rose Harris in 1963; 'Develop or die' warned Rena Stratford in 1964. These words seem to have been effective as netball is flourishing at all levels. The continued success has meant that the rules must be reviewed at regular intervals to ensure that the game remains exciting and skilful. Within the International Federation of Netball Associations there are now thirty-nine countries and this continues to grow each year as netball's popularity steadily increases.

The spread of the game internationally together with the introduction of prestigious world-stage events, has led to a greater need to improve the skill level and tactical play of the competitors. Coaching has become very important and the physical and mental preparation of the players has taken on a greater significance. The game has most certainly moved out of the playground and is in a constant state of development. Visits to the British Isles by teams from Australia, New Zealand, West Indies, South Africa and the Cook Islands, with their differing style of play, have helped inspire young players to try to improve all facets of their game. I hope that this book will also help them and their club coaches everywhere to continue to strive to raise the standards so that the game continues to be played at the highest possible level throughout the world.

1 Fundamentals of the Game

PLAYING NETBALL

Netball is played by two teams of seven players on a court measuring 30.5m (100ft) by 15.25m (50ft). The aim of the game is to keep possession of the ball until it is caught inside a semi-circular marked area, the goal-circle. Only two players in the team are allowed to enter this circle and they are called the goal shooter (GS) and the goal attack (GA). From a position inside the goal-circle they attempt to shoot the ball through a ring suspended on a 3.05m (10ft) goal-post positioned at the centre of the goal-line. The opposing team attempts to intercept

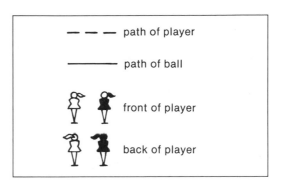

Key.

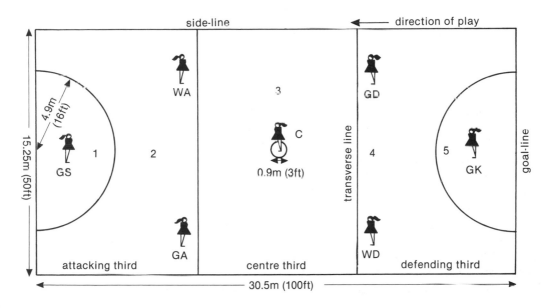

Fig 2   Court plan, playing positions and areas of play.

the ball and when successful tries to keep possession in order to reach its own goal-circle (which is at the opposite end of the court) to attempt to score a goal. The team scoring the most goals is the winner. The game normally lasts for one hour, the teams changing ends after each quarter.

The game is made more difficult by restricting the playing areas of each player. In order to do this the court is divided into thirds by two transverse lines across the court (see Fig 2). The ball must be caught, or at least touched, in each third, so ensuring that netball is a team-game and cannot be dominated by one star-player. Each player has a specific part to play and so each position requires different skills. Further regulations include the footwork rule which restricts movement when in possession of the ball (see page 21) and a three-second time-limit when holding the ball. Netball is, however, easy to play and is exciting when played by very skilful players.

Each player has a restricted area of play as illustrated in Fig 2. If a player goes outside her restricted area she is ruled to be offside. The game is stopped and restarted with a free pass by the opposing team, which is taken in the offside area. A team is allowed to make three substitutions. These substitutions can be made during an interval or to replace a player on court in the case of injury or illness. A player who has been substituted may return to the court providing that she is one of the three permitted substitutions.

Starting the Game *(Fig 3)*

The game is started by the centre of one team attempting to pass the ball to her team-mates from the centre circle (a circle of 0.9m (3ft) diameter, marked in the middle of the court). The player must either receive within the centre court section or catch as she jumps from that section. The opponents will obviously try to prevent this from happening by strong defending. This centre pass is taken alternately by each team after each goal is scored, the first centre pass being determined by the toss of a coin. The team which wins the toss has the choice of either taking the first centre pass or choosing in which direction to play. If the team chooses the direction of play then the opponents would take the first centre pass. At the start of play only the centres from each team can be in the centre area (see the area marked 3 in Fig 2). The other players are free to move within their playing areas but the transverse lines may not be crossed, even by those players allowed to do so, until after the whistle has been blown.

Equipment

The great advantage of the game of netball is that it does not require a large quantity of equipment. Whether playing indoors or

Playing positions		Areas of play
Goal Shooter	– GS	1 & 2
Goal Attack	– GA	1, 2 & 3
Wing Attack	– WA	2 & 3
Centre	– C	2, 3 & 4
Wing Defence	– WD	3 & 4
Goal Defence	– GD	3, 4 & 5
Goalkeeper	– GK	4 & 5

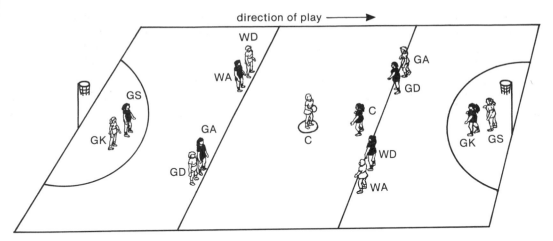

direction of play ⟶

WD
WA
GS
GK
GA
GD
C
C
GA
GD
WD
WA
GK
GS

Fig 3   Start of play, white centre pass.

Fig 4   The well-dressed netball player.

outdoors the surface should be hard and non-slip. The goal-posts can be sunk into a socket in the ground or supported in a base, which should not protrude on to the court. The ring should be 380mm (15in) in diameter and have a net attached. The ball used should be regulation size 5 and made of leather, composite rubber or of other approved materials. Non-leather balls are obviously cheaper and so are available for use with younger players and for practice when many balls may be required.

Over the years the dress of the players has not changed to any great extent (Fig 4). An easy-fitting shirt and short skirt or tunic is the normal dress, although some players choose to wear shorts. Thick socks and training shoes with good grips are necessary because of the sudden starting and stopping required in the course of the game. A jumper may also be required in cold weather, and a track suit to keep the body warm whilst warming up before the game and afterwards whilst cooling down. Distinguishing bibs with marked playing positions are worn by each member of each team. Many teams now wear the letters indicating their playing positions as patches which attach to the shirts and are equally easily removed if the player is substituted. Essentially the playing kit should be loose and comfortable and all team members should be wearing identical outfits; this makes the task of the umpires much easier.

The Umpires

The game is controlled by two umpires who are responsible for ensuring that the players play within the accepted rules as set down by the governing body. In England this is the AENA.

The Captain of the Team

The captain is an important member of the team and has several responsibilities. Some of these are listed below:

(i)   tossing the coin to decide who will have the first centre pass;
(ii) informing the umpires of this decision
(iii) informing the umpires and opposing team captain of any positional change or substitutions;
(iv) discussing any rule difficulty with the umpire at any interval, if required;
(v) thanking her opponents and the umpires at the end of the game.

Sportsmanship

Netball should be played skilfully and sometimes aggressively but always in good spirit. At the end of the game the handshakes and the three calls of cheers to each team help to calm tempers and create friendships with opponents which very often last for a lifetime. Many ex-international players can tell you of the friends they have throughout the world, all of whom were very competitive opponents on the court. Netball is a game to be enjoyed and it is to hoped that this book will be a help to players and coaches alike. It will also help them to develop their skills so that they are able to enjoy highly competitive play as well as creating friendships which last a lifetime.

Summary
- There are seven players in a netball team but only two players can score goals, the goal shooter and the goal attack.
- A full game lasts for one hour and is divided into four quarters with an interval at the end of each quarter.
- A court is divided into three equal parts by two transverse lines. The ball must be caught or touched in each third of the court.
- Goal posts are 3.05m high and can be sunk into the ground or supported by bases.
- Playing uniform must include identifying initials to indicate playing positions.
- Captains toss a coin to see who should take the first centre pass and in which direction a team should play.
- The game starts with a centre pass taken by the centre from the centre circle. The first pass must be either received within the centre court or caught by a player who jumps from that area. Centre passes are taken alternately after a goal has been scored.
- Goals can only be scored from within the goal circles.
- A game is controlled by two umpires.

2 Essential Skills

BALL CONTROL

When learning to play netball the most important skill is the ability to handle and control the ball properly. All early skills practice should be aimed at ensuring the player becomes familiar with the shape, texture, size and weight of the ball. As mentioned in Chapter 1, netball is played with a size 5 ball which is normally made of leather but possibly of synthetic materials. Ideally, experienced players should practise with a regulation size ball but younger players can use a smaller size, as long as it is too large to be gripped by one hand.

Ball control is about sensitivity and feel which, if achieved, appears to tie the ball to the end of a player's fingers. It is also the ability to bring the ball under control when it appears to be completely out of reach. Players who have this control in their fingertips also seem to have it throughout their body and it shows in their footwork, lightness in their landing and balance when catching or throwing the ball. The experienced netball player should have acquired her handling skills in a fun way at an early age, but it is a skill that needs constant reinforcement and should always be included as an integral part of any warm-up session. Here are some practices to try; all you need is a ball and some space. Start each one slowly but as you improve, increase your speed – remember that the main aim of these practices is to have fun.

Sensitivity and Feeling Practices

1. Gentle passing from hand to hand. Begin close together and as you progress gradually widen the distance between your hands. Spread your fingers wide and pass the ball softly; aim for completely silent movement.
2. Begin passing hand to hand as for Practice 1, but gradually make the ball travel further so that the player's feet have to move to the side. Maintain the softness and sensitivity at the point of catching.
3. Continue hand to hand passing but, now the ball is thrown from a position in front of the body over the head in a forwards and backwards movement. Retain your sensitivity of touch by bending your back, so ensuring the ball is caught softly.
4. Individually, support the ball on your hand over your head with your fingers pointing backwards (see Fig 5). From this position do each of the following:

(a) twist your hand and lower to bring the ball in front of the body. Practise using your right hand initially and then your left hand (see Fig 6);
(b) flick the ball into the air, catch it while it is still overhead with your fingers back and twist your hand to bring the ball down in front of your body. Remember to aim for sensitivity and softness so there is no noise as your hand touches the ball; give through your whole body – through your fingers, arms, trunk and knees.
(c) again flick the ball into the air, but this

Fig 5   Support ball, fingers pointing backwards.

Fig 6   Twist hand to support the ball in front.

time jump to meet it. Control the ball and bring it down with as much sensitivity as possible.

5. Throw the ball into the air, forwards, sideways or backwards and each time move your feet in order to be able to jump and bring the ball down with a twisting action of the hand. Try to ensure a softness on contact and place your second hand on the ball as soon as possible to achieve controlled possession.

6. Be aware of the speed of the ball as you do the following practices:

(a) throw the ball into the air and reach up to meet it as it falls. Catch it by moving one hand down at the side of the ball at the same speed and then twisting

under to catch. Quickly bring your second hand on to the ball to gain control. Feel the give through your whole body – from the fingers to the trunk, to the knees. Aim for a softness of touch;
(b) as for (a) but jump to meet the ball;
(c) bounce the ball hard and catch as in exercise (a) and (b) but as the ball is falling back to the ground. Watch the ball carefully and try to catch it by twisting either as close to the ground as possible or as close to the top of the bounce as possible.
(d) from a bounce, catch the ball by placing your hand on the top of it whilst it is at the top of its bounce. Twist down the side and under the ball to gain control. Remember to place your other hand as quickly as possible in order to secure complete possession;

Figs 8 & 9   Handling and mobility practice as the ball travels around the waist and the ankles.

Fig 7   Pull the ball away from the opponent.

(e) as for (d) but this time use the technique to retrieve a loose ball. Throw the ball out in front, side or behind you and catch after the first bounce. Pull the ball back to your body after moving, stretching out and twisting your hand round the ball. Try this with a partner to see who gains possession first. (*See* Fig 7.)

Hand and Finger Work Together with Body Suppleness Practices

1.   Make the ball travel around your body, to the left and then right, keeping one hand in contact with the ball throughout. Make the ball travel down to your ankles and up round your neck with continual movement. You may move your body to make it easier. (*See* Figs 8 and 9.)

Fig 9.

2. Make the ball travel in a figure of eight through your legs while standing feet astride.

3. Holding the ball in one hand, take the ball behind your back and flick it into the air. With a quick twisting movement of your body, catch the ball with the opposite hand and then with the same hand.

4. Hold the ball on top of your hand. Turn it under your arm and push upwards, returning to the original position with a quick twist of your hand. The ball should be balanced on top of your hand throughout. Try this on your other hand!

5. Allow the ball to run down your arm from your shoulder and catch it safely as the ball runs over your hands and fingers. Give through your body at the same speed as the ball is moving.

Figs 10–12 Spinning the ball with hands, fingers, and even with one hand.

6. With your legs astride, support the ball between your legs with one hand in front of the body and one behind. Release the ball and quickly twist to change hands to catch the ball before it has reached the ground. Do this on the spot and then try it on the move.

7. Hold the ball on top of your hand and quickly turn your hand around the ball and catch it without losing contact.

8. Hold the ball above your head with your fingers pointing backwards. Spin the ball by using loose, floppy wrists and fingers. Move your feet in order to stay under the ball at all times. Begin by using both hands together and then either your left or right hand or one after the other as illustrated in Figs 10, 11 and 12.

9. Practise controlled bouncing of the ball using your hands to press down on the ball but with no slapping noise. Use both hands together, then your left or right hand alternately. Move your feet to keep up with the ball and travel round with it. You may use skittles to mark out a route.

Fig 11.

10. Bounce the ball as suggested in the following exercise variations:

(a) around your body keeping your feet still and changing hands;
(b) pivoting your body whilst keeping one foot on the ground all the time;
(c) between your legs – side to side, back to front, figure of eight.
(d) turning and catching the ball before it bounces again;
(e) running to touch a wall or line and catching it before it bounces again;
(f) sit down, throw the ball over your head, get up and catch it before the second bounce;
(g) lie down and repeat variation (f);
(h) see how many bounces you can do in one minute;

(i) see how few bounces you can do in one minute.

Practices for Two Players with One or Two Balls

1. Player A holds the ball and faces B. She passes the ball around her ankles, then her waist and then her neck before passing it on to her partner who repeats these activities.
2. A and B repeat Exercise 1 each with a ball. Their aim is to keep the balls moving smoothly while interchanging the balls, going as fast as possible to try to be the first to be ready to exchange her ball.
3. A and B face each other, first gently volleying the ball using both hands, then right hand to right hand, and finally, left to left. Each player should concentrate on relaxing and pushing from the wrists aiming for a smooth, quiet action.
4. Using two balls and facing each other, A and B keep both balls moving with A's right hand passing to her partner's left and her left receiving from her partner's right as in Fig 13.

These practices are fun and can easily be adapted if there are not enough balls. The training can be done inside or outside, as individual self-challenges, as group activities or even as team races. My experience has been that players enjoy performing these exercises and that all learning gained in this way is carried over into other skill activities – the player with good handling skills stands out in any team.

FOOTWORK

An important skill which can be acquired early is good footwork. This does not only mean knowledge and application of the

Fig 12.

15

Fig 13   A study in concentration.

footwork rule (the rule which limits the movement of the player in possession of the ball, *see* page 21), it means the ability of the player to run, to stop, to change direction, to jump and to land safely. All these attributes demand an awareness of body balance and control. Good footwork control forms the basis for getting away from your opponent to receive a pass or getting close enough to mark her and make it possible to intercept an attempted pass. Superior footwork demands physical fitness and suppleness and ensures you are agile and mobile throughout the whole of the match.

Individual Practices

1. All players should jog easily around the court. Each player should keep her body relaxed and her eyes watching the other players.

2. Again with all players on the court jogging easily, each player should move anywhere within the court being aware of the other players' movements, moving smoothly in and out to avoid any contact.

3. Repeat Exercise 2 but reduce the court space, possibly use only one-third of the court. Each player should keep control, with their feet very much under their body so they are able to react quickly and smoothly whenever required.

4. Continue Exercise 3 but the players are numbered either one or two. If their number is called they move smoothly in and out of the remaining standing players who become obstacles to avoid. When the other number is called, the first number called stands still. Be aware

16

of how other players are avoiding the obstacles. Are they swerving or stopping and moving sideways or changing direction? Observation of their feet for ease and speed of movement is also helpful.

5. Using the length of the court each player should try these various exercises:

(a) jog the first third, sidestep the middle third and jog the last third;
(b) jog the first third, stride the middle third and jog the last third;
(c) jog the first third, skip the second third with high knee-lifts and jog to the end;
(d) jog the first third, twist and turn placing one foot in front and then behind the leading leg whilst travelling sideways through the middle third and jog to the end;
(e) jog the first third, hop the middle third, changing legs half way and jog to the end;
(f) jog the first third, sprint the middle third and jog to the end;
(g) jog the first third, turn and travel backwards over the middle third, turn and jog to the end.

6. To improve a player's movement over all of the court the circuits shown in Figs 14 and 15 should be practised regularly.

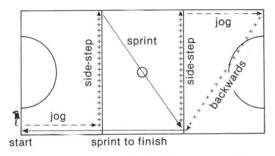

Fig 14   Circuit to encourage varied footwork patterns.

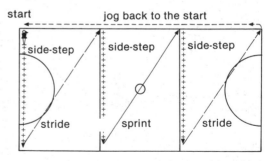

Fig 15   Circuit to encourage varied footwork patterns.

7. Each player should continue to improve her footwork by running using the lines on the court in the following ways:

(a) run and stop at lines;
(b) run and change direction at lines;
(c) run and when you meet someone on your line make a quick change of direction.

8. Running between two lines, two or three metres apart, each player should:

(a) practise short side-steps, widening the last step at the line to change direction;
(b) practise short side-steps, reaching to touch the line with the opposite hand to the foot nearest to the line.

9. Pivoting exercises should be carried out in the following variations:

(a) pivoting on either foot using the other foot as balance;
(b) pivot on one foot and running forward by pushing off from the pivoting foot;
(c) running, stopping and pivoting at every line met;
(d) running along the marked lines, pivoting at every line junction;

17

(e) running, jumping and pivoting on the landing foot, use the second foot to change direction and run off somewhere else.

Practices in Pairs

1. Pair up with another player and try to stand on your partner's toes. She must avoid this by employing quick foot movements.
2. Your partner should have a coloured band tucked into the back of her skirt; you must try to retrieve this with some quick footwork.
3. One partner leads and the other follows within a confined space. The leader tries to change the pace and direction as often as possible to try to lose the follower, who must try to keep up with her.
4. Face your partner and try to stay with her as she *chassé* steps (takes gliding steps) from side to side.
5. This time start behind your partner and try to stay with her as you repeat Practice 4.
6. One follows the other across the court, both jogging. The back player touches the front player who sprints to the far side of the court; try to touch her again before she gets there.
7. Repeat Practice 6 but as you touch your partner she turns and tries to catch you before you reach the other side of the court.
8. Face your partner who side-steps to prevent you from passing her. You will need excellent footwork to pass her.
9. Face your partner again but stand either side of two skittles placed 1m (3ft) apart. Try to touch your partner without reaching or moving between the skittles.

Practices with Three or More

1. Begin with A, B and C jogging together from the side-line towards the opposite side and then practise the following variations remembering that in each case A and C have to try to beat B back to the line:

(a) B suddenly sprints to the opposite side;
(b) B suddenly stops and returns to the original line;
(c) B suddenly stops and either goes on again or turns and comes back.

2. **Triangle-tag.** A, B and C face each other and hold hands to form a triangle. D is on the outside and tries to touch B as the triangle moves so B is always the furthest away.
3. **Fox and Geese.** With any number of players each standing behind the other holding the waist of the player in front; one free player faces the front person and tries to touch the player at the back of the line.
4. With any number of players jogging in a line with a space between each player, practise these two exercises:

(a) the back player sprints to the front and becomes the leader. Then the new back player sprints to the front and so on;
(b) the back player moves in and out between the players and then becomes the new leader. The new player at the back goes next and so on.

5. With players evenly spaced out down the court and all facing the same way, the front player turns and tries to get all the way down the court by avoiding each player in turn. Each player tries to prevent her by using a side to side movement. Once she gets through the new front player makes her bid to get down the court.

6. Players A, C and E form a line at one side of the court facing B and D on the opposite side. A runs to touch B, B runs to touch C, who runs to touch D and so on. Continue until each player has crossed the court six times.

Advanced Practices I

The quick-changing footwork patterns and the continuous nature of these practices mean that they are good for fitness. A high fitness level can be encouraged by making players work for thirty seconds and then rest for thirty seconds or by making players complete a number of circuits.

1. Use the width of one-third of the court with two added lines, or if indoors a badminton court will do equally as well. (See Fig 16.)
2. Use the centre third of the court. (See Fig 17.)
3. Using four cones, mark out a fan-shaped circuit as shown in Fig 18. You should move around each cone in turn, returning to the base cone after each loop. Organize your body and foot patterns in order to cope with the tight loops.
4. Run a figure of eight with four players. Take up positions as illustrated in Fig 19 so,

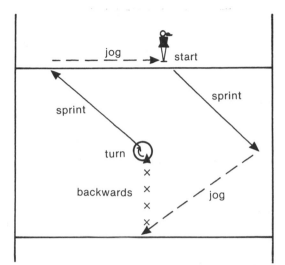

Fig 17 A more game-related footwork drill.

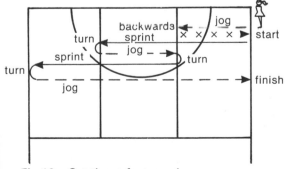

Fig 16 Get those feet moving.

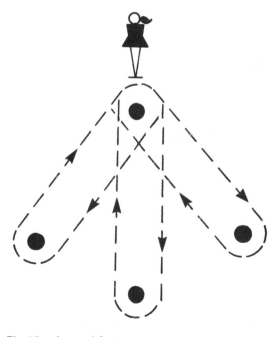

Fig 18 A good foot management exercise; try to keep facing forwards.

19

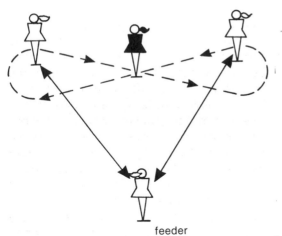

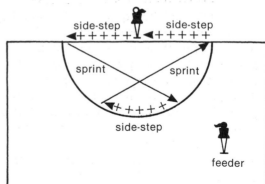

Fig 20   Footwork management encouraging a change of pace.

Fig 19   Training in a figure of eight, but watch the feeder all the time and then make the interception.

as the central player, you can complete a figure of eight around the two outer players while constantly watching the feeder. You intercept the ball when the feeder passes to one of the stationary players and you continue running and pass the ball to the standing player, who returns it to the feeder. Whilst doing the figures of eight watch the person feeding the ball at all times and move to intercept passes.

5. Using the circle area, place five cones or crosses at regular intervals along the whole curve of the circle. A feeder stands holding a ball 3m (10ft) away from the edge of the circle. and facing a player who begins by the goal-post. This player practises the following:

(a) side-steps out and back to each cone or cross in turn;
(b) sprints out and side-steps back;
(c) side-steps out and sprints back.

She must keep her head up at all times and watch the feeder, adapting her footwork to make this possible. These exercises should

be repeated with the feeder passing the ball to the player so that it is caught at the outside of the circle, then at the post, and then progressing to the ball being caught at either or both positions. Each time the ball is caught the player should return it to the feeder and so the circuit continues.
6. Use a circle to encourage changes of speed in footwork. Complete the circuit in Fig 20, always watching the feeder but

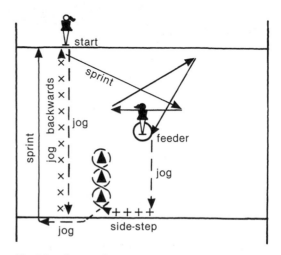

Fig 21   A practice to encourage good footwork and handling as well as good stamina training.

without the ball being thrown. Repeat the circuit with the feeder passing the ball at the end of each sprint. You must learn to cope with the changes of pace as well as with catching and landing at speed.

7. Use a third of the court to continue practising more uses of footwork. Jog a third of the court and then travel backwards to where you started from. Continuing your progress, run diagonally forward to catch the ball to the left of the feeder and return the ball, then catch to the right of the feeder and return the ball. Sprint forward to take a dropped pass from the feeder and return the ball, then jog to the third line and side-step along it. Run in and out between three cones then return to the third line and turn and sprint back to the start.

THE FOOTWORK RULE *(Figs 22–8)*

If players have a good grounding in the use of their feet about the court then they usually do not find the restrictions of the footwork rule too difficult to master. It is, in my opinion, unfairly described as 'the rule that makes you stop when in possession of the ball'. It may look like this when performed by a beginner but the more experienced player, with total command of her body and the footwork rule, can make the whole catching, landing and throwing look very fluid indeed. Very rarely does a player catch the ball when she is standing still. She normally catches the ball in the air, lands on one foot and uses the second foot to control her balance and forward movement. She may move this second or stepping foot several times before stepping forward on it to release the ball. The rule limits the movement of the first or landing foot to either

Figs 22–5 The footwork rule – landing foot, stepping to gain control, pulling back to gain a balanced position and pivoting on landing foot to pass to the side.

Fig 23.

21

Fig 24.

Fig 25.

Figs 26–8   Running footwork –
landing foot, stepping foot, jumping
and releasing the ball before
regrounding the landing foot.

Fig 27.

Fig 28.

pivoting, provided it stays in contact with the ground, or being lifted cleanly, in which case it cannot be regrounded until after the ball has been released. The second or stepping foot may be lifted and grounded as often as is required in order to achieve a balanced throwing position.

Sometimes players land on both feet simultaneously thus giving themselves the choice of which foot to move. The first one to be moved becomes the stepping foot and the normal footwork rule applies. This may be advantageous to shooters as they can choose the nearest foot to the post as their landing foot and therefore achieve a closer shot. In normal court play the one-two landing is much more fluid and gives the player a much greater choice of activity following the landing. Many of the footwork

practices given earlier can be adapted to introduce the rule to young players, particularly the stopping at lines and pivoting practices but a few more are included below.

Early Training

1. Run, jump and land on your right leg, bending your knee as it lands to absorb the shock and then using your left leg to prevent any overbalance. Pull your left foot back towards your right foot in order to achieve a totally balanced position. Repeat this but land on your left foot first.
2. Jog around the court and on a call or whistle, run, jump and land one-two. Thrust your second foot out, in order to help control the forward speed and move this foot as often as possible in order to achieve a balanced position. Try landing on either foot.
3. Continue Practice 2 but land on both feet simultaneously and then move one foot as often as possible to regain a balanced position.
4. Run and jump landing one-two; keep the first foot down but pivot on it by moving the second foot round in order to face another direction. Practise landing on either foot.
5. Throw a ball into the air, jump to catch and land one-two. Pivot round and throw in another direction.
6. In pairs, throw to your partner who jumps to catch landing one-two. She then steps forward to return the ball to you.
7. In threes, A with the ball and B and C facing her on the opposite side of the court. B runs forward to catch a pass from A. She lands one-two, pivots on her landing foot to face C and throws the ball to her. B then continues across the court

taking up a position behind A, who then runs forward to take the pass from C. The practice continues. It can be further developed by B moving out diagonally forward, turning and pivoting on the landing foot to return the ball to C.

It is accepted that players throw better when the landing foot is on the same side of the body as the throwing hand. Young children should therefore be encouraged to land this way when they are learning to throw, but as they become more experienced it is desirable to be able to land on either foot.

Advanced Practices II

1. Continuing to practise in threes, with B and C lined up opposite A, as B moves forward to catch the ball as she turns in the air. As she lands she must cope with her landing footwork before returning the ball to C.
2. Continue Exercise 1 but the player catching lands – right, left – when moving out to her right and – left, right – when moving out to her left.
3. Position a goal-post behind C and repeat the practice but after B throws to C, C lands simultaneously on both feet forward and back. She then turns

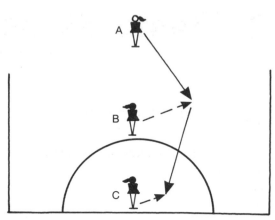

Fig 29   The goal shooter (C) practises the split landing.

towards the post, and back. She then turns towards the post, moves the foot furthest away from the post towards the other and shoots at goal. (*See* Fig 29.)
4. A throws wide to B, making B move out quickly. As she catches the ball B thrusts her foot forward, controls her balance, turns and steps on to her second foot, lifting her landing foot and passes the ball wide to C. By this time C has moved to the side – she catches, lands one-two or simultaneously, turns and shoots, using the correct footwork. Practise this exercise with players moving out either side.

Summary
- The ability to control the body and the ball forms the basis for good netball play. Both should be practised at every opportunity. These are fundamental skills and need to be learnt at an early age.
- Players should learn to move easily using sprints, jogs and side-steps and should be equally at home when moving in any direction. Balance is very important and should be stressed at all times.
- Players should be given every opportunity to handle a netball and should be encouraged to discover their own powers of control through fun and juggling activities.
- Learning the Footwork Rule requires a good control of balance.
- All players should be able to land on one foot or both feet and should learn to turn in the air before landing, and to use the pivot to change direction after landing.
- The basic skills of netball are based on an understanding of the Footwork Rule.

3 Basic Skills

CATCHING *(Figs 30–3)*

The ability to catch follows on quite naturally from the earlier ball-handling practices. Catching means developing safe hands, the ability to retain hold of the ball whether it has been very wide or very hard or when under pressure from your opponents. In order to catch safely the player must be able to judge the speed of the ball and the direction of its flight. The aim of the player is to catch the ball and to bring it into the comparative safety of a 'holding' position – a position in front of the chest and close to the body. From this position the ball can be on the move again very quickly and so be released within the statutory three seconds. Good catching involves:

(i) the eyes, watch and judge the flight and speed of the ball as it approaches the player;
(ii) the arms, reach out towards the ball with your arms at full stretch;
(iii) the hands, spread your fingers out wide making a receiving cup with your thumbs at the back to prevent the ball from slipping through. As it hits the fin-

Fig 30 Sue Collins of England catches safely under pressure from New Zealand.

Fig 31 The ideal 'holding' position.

gers, let your hands give in the line of the flight of the throw;

(iv) the body, continue this cushioning effect by giving through the arms and the body, gradually coping with the pace and the power of the throw;

(v) the feet, bending at the hips, knees and ankles on landing will complete the catch and ensure a strong balanced base for the following throw. This may involve dropping one foot backwards (normally the right foot in right-handed throwers), in order to cope with the pace of the throw and then transferring the weight back on to the front foot after the power has been dissipated. Catching with one hand should only be done when safe two-handed catching is not possible. This may be when the ball is very wide of the catcher, is possibly

Fig 33   Cushioning the catch to take the pace off the ball.

outside the boundary of the court or has rebounded off the goal-post into a position where it is impossible to get two hands to the ball. The principles of good catching are the same but the ball should be very quickly brought from the one-handed catching position into the more secure two-handed holding position.

As players become more skilful the time between the catch and the release of the throw becomes much less and although they may still move through the 'holding' position, the stop which is encouraged in learners may disappear totally, the 'giving' of the catch becoming the preparation for the throw.

Early Practices

Much of the early experience in catching should be learned from the ball-handling

Fig 32   Reaching out to receive the ball.

skills of Chapter 2, where the softness and sensitivity are encouraged and players learn to cope with the ball travelling at various speeds and strengths. Here are a few more practices to encourage good catching – working in pairs for the next four exercises:

1. The thrower passes the ball towards the catcher who reaches forward with her fingers spread. As the ball hits her hands it is brought back towards her body, the weight of her body is moved on to her back foot which cushions the speed of the ball. The weight is then transferred forward on to the front foot so returning to a balanced holding position. Take it in turns to be the thrower or the catcher. The thrower should increase the pace and power of the throw as the skill increases.

Fig 34   A full stretch to take the high ball.

2. The catcher stands with her feet comfortably spaced, elbows tucked in and arms ready for action. The thrower passes the ball above the catcher's head who extends to full-stretch to catch the ball (see Fig 34). She lands, grounding one foot before the other. The ball is pulled into a controlled holding position before the player steps forward on to the foot that was grounded last and passes the ball back to the thrower.

3. The catcher stands in the alert position as practised previously. The thrower passes the ball to the right of the catcher who thrusts off with her left foot and extends to catch the ball. She lands on the right foot with the left foot still off the ground. The ball is pulled in towards the body and as the weight is transferred back on to the left foot, the ball is returned to the thrower as illustrated in Figs 35–7. This is repeated by throwing to her left side.

4. The thrower stands in front of the catcher facing a wall. She throws the ball against the wall so that it rebounds to the left or to the right. The catcher moves to the appropriate side, catches the rebound and still lands in a controlled and balanced position. By starting with the catcher in front of the thrower this practice can be used to quicken the catcher's reactions even more.

Advanced Practices

1. Working with three or more players; the thrower passes the ball to the right of the catcher who runs and extends her hands towards the ball. As she catches the ball she thrusts her right foot forward as the landing foot, pivots round on that foot and steps on to her left foot to pass the ball on to the third player positioned behind her at the start. During the catch

27

Figs 35–7 The wing defence is ready to move to her right, takes the catch landing on the right foot and pulls back to the centre to return the ball to her feeder.

Fig 36.

Fig 37.

the ball is pulled in to the chest and then passed on. With further practice the catcher will begin to turn in the air and then will be able to pass the ball without the need for the pivot. The catcher then moves behind the original thrower who now moves forward to take the next catch. An alternative practice can be done with the catcher moving out to the left.

2. In pairs; the thrower passes the ball so wide to the catcher's right that the catcher must extend only one hand. She catches and quickly returns the ball to the two-handed safe position, at the same time coping with the landing and eventual return of the ball to the thrower. Repeat this exercise with the catcher moving out to the left.

3. Repeat Practice 1 but with one-handed catching and turning.

4. In pairs; with the catcher standing close to a side-line, the thrower passes the ball so it travels in the air over the side-line. The catcher reaches out (*see* Fig 38) with one

Fig 38   Keep your body-weight over your right foot.

29

Fig 39 Pull the ball away from your opponent.

Fig 40 Returning the ball into play before landing outside the court.

hand, catches the ball and safely holds it with two hands before throwing it back to the thrower. Try this with the catcher standing still and then jumping to catch. Remember she must not go out of court. Practise using either hand.

5. In threes; the thrower passes the ball into the air between the other two players; they try to catch the ball by jumping to catch with one hand (see Fig 39). The first to the ball quickly pulls it away from the other player and brings it safely into her two hands ready to pass back to the thrower.

6. In threes, a shooter and two catchers; the two catchers compete to catch the rebound from the shooter's attempted shot. They must not go out of court.

7. Working in pairs; the thrower passes the ball and as it begins to go out of court,

the catcher jumps and attempts to catch it, and return it into the court area before she lands and makes contact with the out of court area as shown in Fig 40. Practise this using either hand.

THE TOSS-UP

The toss-up is another means of winning possession of the ball. It is awarded when two opposing players either catch the ball at the same time, deflect the ball out of court at the same time, break a rule at the same time or when the umpire is unable to make a decision. It is a fair means of putting the ball back into play as it gives either side an equal opportunity to gain possession. It is used quite often in a game and therefore is a useful skill to have acquired through practice. Any player may be involved in a toss-up and therefore all members of the team should practise trying to gain possession.

The two players involved stand facing each other and their own attacking end. Their arms must be held straight and by their sides. They can stand with feet together or one foot in front of the other, but there must be a distance of 0.9m (3ft) between the nearer foot of either player. It is the umpire's job to see that the players are positioned correctly. She puts the ball back into play by flicking the ball up between the players from a position below the shoulder level of the smaller player. As she does this she blows her whistle; this is the signal for the players to move. They normally try to catch the ball but are also allowed to tip or bat the ball, as long as this is not directed straight at the umpire or the opponent. Catching of the ball requires very quick reactions and these can be learned.

Early Practices

1. All players stand still with their knees slightly bent, arms by their sides but with their hands and fingers alert. On the whistle each player instantly claps her hands.
2. In pairs; hold the ball on the palm of your hand and face your partner, who takes up the normal toss-up position. On the whistle, she swings her arms quickly forward to take the ball off your hand and quickly pulls the ball back towards her body and into the holding position. She should experiment with pulling the ball upwards and over her shoulder and turning away from you to protect the ball.
3. Vary Exercise 2 with A, the player holding the ball, blowing a whistle and at the same time flicking the ball up into the air but not more than 0.6m (2ft) above her partner's shoulder level.
4. In threes with one player as the umpire and two taking part in the toss-up as in Fig 41. The umpire stands equidistant between

Fig 41   The toss-up.

the players and checks that they are standing correctly and the required distance apart. The umpire blows the whistle and at the same time flicks the ball up into the air; the two players compete for the ball.

Advanced Practices

1. Practise in fours; two are involved in the toss-up, one is the umpire and the fourth player waits ready to receive the pass from the player who successfully gains possession of the ball.
2. Practise in sixes; with C as the umpire. If A wins the ball at the toss-up she passes to her team-mate D who then passes on to F. If B wins the toss-up she passes to her team-mate E and then on to F. At the toss-up E may defend D or vice versa depending on whose team-mate is successful at winning the ball. Eventually encourage the unsuccessful player at the toss-up to also defend the pass to D or E, provided that she is the correct distance away from the thrower, 0.9m (3ft). (See Fig 42.)

BATTING AND CATCHING

Sometimes the ball is just out of reach for a successful catch to be made without making contact with an opponent. In cases like these it may be necessary to deflect the ball into a place where it can be caught more easily or where it can be caught by a team-mate. The arm is still extended towards the ball but as contact is made a movement of the wrist redirects the ball into an open space or towards a team-mate. This may be done with either hand and may send the ball into the air or down on to the ground. In either case it is a deliberate movement and so more than an undirected tip. But remember a player is only allowed to bat the ball once before gaining possession.

Early Practices

1. Each player stands facing a wall so she is close enough to touch it. Using a strong wrist action to keep the ball bouncing against the wall and using both left and right hands, each player begins by keeping the ball above head-height and gradually develops this skill to keep the ball moving on the wall in an arc from left to right side and back again.
2. Working in pairs; the thrower passes the ball to the right of the catcher, who reaches out and bats the ball down on to the ground before catching the rebound. Repeat this to the left side.
3. In threes, A, B and C. Start with A throwing the ball high into the air above B and C. They both jump and compete to gain possession by reaching and batting the ball with one hand into a place where they can catch it more easily.
4. Working in threes, stand in a triangle about 5m (15ft) apart. A passes the ball between B and C, B moves and reaches out to bat the ball on to C, who then passes the next pass between A and B, with A batting the ball on to B. The practice

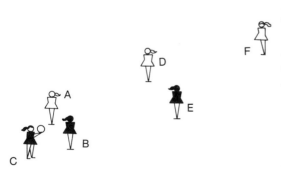

Fig 42   The toss-up and movement after.

continues around the triangle. The practice should also be reversed.

Advanced Practices

1. Working in a triangle 2m (6ft), A and B have a ball each. They take turns to pass their ball to one side of C who moves from side to side using smooth and rhythmic footwork, returning the ball by batting using her hand nearest to the thrower.

2. Positioned as for Exercise 1; A throws the ball in front of B and C who move forward to try to bat the ball into a safe place to gain possession.

3. A is the thrower and she passes the ball towards B who is facing her. C moves in from the right of the intended catcher B and reaches across in front using her right hand to bat the ball away without any body contact (*see* Fig 43). C then continues through in order to gain possession of the ball. This practice should be tried from the left also and can be made more difficult by C approaching from a position behind B.

4. With A as the thrower again, she passes a high ball to to B. At the same time C moves quickly backwards from a starting position between the two players and tries to bat the ball over the head of the intended catcher as seen in Fig 44. She may have more success if she turns her hand towards B when trying to make contact.

5. Continue Exercise 4 but C makes the decision to catch or bat the ball depending on its height. A catch is to be encouraged, but if a catch cannot be made without making contact with the

Fig 43 Batting using the hand furthest away to avoid any contact.

Fig 44 Note the turning of the hand.

intended catcher then batting should be chosen.

THROWING

The easiest ball to catch safely is one that is thrown accurately, at the correct speed and into the right place so it is within easy reach of the catcher but out of reach of her opponent. The catch should become the preparation for the next throw. In the early stages of training, players should be encouraged to have a slight stop in their holding position to give them time to control their balance and make decisions regarding who to throw to, how fast the player is moving and what type of throw will reach her most successfully. The more skilful and experienced player will be able to cope with all of this without the need to pause in the holding position and the catch and the throw will merge together producing a smooth movement without any break.

There are many ways of throwing the ball, but whichever type of throw is chosen each involves three common stages:

(i)   a preparation stage; when the ball will be moved from the holding position to the point where it is to begin to move towards the target;

(ii)   a release stage; when the ball will be directed in the chosen direction by the movement of the body, the arms and the fingers;

(iii)   a follow-through stage; which will vary in length according to the power needed for the throw.

A successful throwing technique greatly depends on the use of good footwork. The ideal position would be a balanced one, with one foot forward and one foot back. As the throw is made the weight is transferred from the back foot, ideally the landing foot, to the front foot, the stepping foot. The release of the ball and the follow-through coincide with this foot movement. The step should be made in the direction of the throw and the length of the stride will vary depending on the length of the throw; a longer stride being required for a long throw. Whenever possible the stepping should be on the opposite side to the throwing arm, but more experienced players will be able to adapt according to how they have landed.

The Shoulder Pass (Figs 45–7)

The shoulder pass is the most effective method of delivering a long accurate

Figs 45–7   The shoulder pass – ready for action – in the holding position.

Fig 46 Ball and body moved into the throwing position, sideways on and weight over the back foot.

Fig 47 A strong push forward and follow-through, body-weight transferred on to the forward foot.

pass and as such forms the basis of the English game. The player stands sideways to the target with her feet shoulder-width apart and her weight over her back foot. The ball is taken from the holding position to a position behind her body and at head-height, with her fingers spread out behind the ball. Her eyes should be fixed on the target as the ball is projected forward via her shoulders, elbow, wrist and fingers. As this is done her weight is transferred from her back foot and is thrust forward on to her leading foot. Her hips should also turn towards the target as the ball is released. Her hand stays in contact with the ball for as long as possible, in order to ensure accuracy and so continues to follow-through in the direction of the throw after the ball is released. The throw must be completed within three seconds.

The Chest Pass *(Figs 48 & 49)*

The chest pass is a two-handed pass delivered from the chest region. Its advantage is that it is a very quick pass as the holding position and the release position are so close together. It is also very easy to foint a pass before releasing in another direction. The pass begins with the holding position, the ball being held close to the chest with the fingers at either side of the ball and the thumbs at the back. The ball is moved sharply forward, the elbows straightening and the fingers and thumbs giving the final push and follow-through after the release of the ball. If possible the bodyweight should be transferred on to the leading foot but this is not essential as it is normally a short distance pass.

With practice the pass can also be made from the side of the body (*see* Figs

Figs 48 & 49   The chest pass – fingers spread, thumbs behind the ball.

Fig 49   Elbows straighten and fingers give that final push.

Fig 51.

Figs 50 & 51   The side pass – hands turned, followed by a strong release.

50 and 51), although this will require a turning of the body and also a turning of the hands so that they are on top and below the ball as it is released. The direction of the pass can also be varied, so it is straight, high in a lob or downwards on

to the ground as a bounce pass. In each case the follow-through is short and in the direction of the throw.

The Overhead Pass or Lob
(Figs 52–4)

The overhead pass is a two-handed pass delivered from above the head and is used as a means of lifting the ball over the head of an opponent and yet reaching the intended catcher at an easy catching height. The ball is held in the holding position and is quickly taken to a position over the head where it is held with elbows bent, fingers on either side of the ball and thumbs at the rear. The wrists drop slightly down behind the head

before the arms, wrists and fingers fully extend to give a high release point. If necessary, extra power can be gained by the body-weight being transferred forward at the same time, but this is not often needed as this tends to be a precision pass over a short area when balance and control are more important than power. The follow-through is very short and is mainly in the movement of the wrists.

This throw can be adapted if you step back whenever your opponent is too close in front of you or by jumping and releasing the ball above and over your defending opponent. The trajectory of the pass can also vary according to your requirements; it may start high and stay at that level, or it may be more of a lob

Figs 52 & 53   The overhead pass – wrists drop, then arms, wrists and fingers straighten.

Fig 53.

which lifts over your opponent and drops into a catchable position for your receiver. The overhead pass is essentially one that needs a lot of practice in order to ensure it is always accurate and precise.

The Underarm Pass *(Figs 55 & 56)*

The underarm pass is a one-handed pass, delivered from below the waist and is used as a means of passing the ball to a player who is fairly close and not marked, or as a means of passing the ball below the outstretched arms of a defending opponent. The player has the ball in both hands in the holding position and then quickly moves it downwards and backwards to a position below hip height. The ball is turned so that it is supported by her hand underneath the ball. Her fingers are

Figs 55 & 56   The underarm pass – the ball is delivered with the hand underneath.

Fig 54   The jump pass up and over your opponent.

Fig 56   Her weight moves forward as her arm swings.

spread and as her body weight is transferred from her back to her front foot her steadying hand on top of the ball is removed and her arm holding the ball is swung forward and the ball is released from her fingers in a low position in front of her body. Her delivery stride is long and her fingers stay in contact with the ball as long as possible in order to ensure the accuracy of the delivery. The follow-through also tends to be long and smooth.

The Bounce and the Drop Pass
(Figs 57 –61)

The bounce and the drop pass are passes that defenders find most difficult to intercept. They can be delivered with one or both hands, either from a position in front of, or from the side of, or from very wide of the body. In all these cases the aim is to make sure the ball passes the defender at a difficult height for her to catch and yet finishes at an accessible height and space to be caught by the attacking player. The two-handed bounce is the strongest pass but the one-handed bounce and the drop pass give a wider choice of release. The bounce pass should reach the catcher at about hip-height whereas the drop pass is delivered into a space protected by the attacker and should not rise too far from the ground. Understanding the footwork rule increases the ability of the thrower to put the ball into this protected space. The two-handed bounce is delivered with the hands at the side of the ball, the one-handed bounce with the hand at the back of the ball and the drop pass with the hand underneath the ball, but in all cases the ball begins in the

Fig 57 The bounce is used to beat the defending opponent.

Fig 58 The bounce pass – two hands hold the ball at the side.

39

Fig 59   Hands, fingers and thumbs direct the ball downwards.

Fig 60   The bounce pass using one hand.

Fig 61   The sympathetic drop pass carefully dropped into the protected space.

safety of the holding position and then is moved to the point of release.

Making Decisions about Throwing

With all these types of throws available the attacking player must be able to make good quick decisions. Her choice will depend on:

(i)   the distance the receiver is from her own position;
(ii) how fast the receiver is moving;
(iii) the space around her and immediately available;
(iv) where her opponent is positioned;
(v)   how fast the opponent is moving.

It would be of little use if she threw the ball outside the boundaries of the court. She must decide where to throw, when to throw and which type of throw will prove most successful. All this must be done within three seconds and that is why netball is such a skilful game. Young players will quite often make the wrong choice, not only of the type of throw but also the choice of the best-placed player to receive the pass. With more experience, players will learn to choose wisely.

Decision Making

GUIDANCE DURING PLAY

1. Take your time as you catch the ball, stay balanced and look ahead to see which of your team-mates is in a position to receive your throw.
2. If they are moving, decide how fast they are moving and where they are moving. If you think it is out to the side, prepare to throw to the side and ahead of them. If you think it is away from you, prepare to throw over the defender into a space that your team-mate will reach first. If you decide it is directly towards you, prepare to throw straight at them. In each case use the most appropriate type of throw to achieve your aim.
3. If they are standing but protecting a space, use the correct footwork and type of throw to put the ball safely into that protected space.
4. Be aware of your opponent's positions. If she is in front of the catcher, prepare to use a lob. Should she be behind, use a more direct chest pass which will give her too little time to move round. If she is defending from one side, throw towards the unmarked side.

GUIDANCE IN A DEADBALL SITUATION

There are many times during the game when it needs to be restarted from a still position; using either a centre pass, a throw-in, a free pass or a penalty pass. The umpire will restart the game by blowing her whistle, calling 'play' or by acknowledging that the player is in the correct position. Remember that the three seconds time limit begins from his moment.

1. Use the time while you either move to pick up the ball, enter the centre circle or step up to the line, to look around and begin to make decisions on which of your players are more favourably placed.
2. Take note of where your team-mates' opponents are. Observe whether they are in front, behind or at the side, or if they are hanging-off inviting the pass so that they can make an interception.
3. Take note of where your opponent is. Decide whether she is close and therefore likely to interfere with your throw or if she is standing off with the intention of trying to prevent your throw reaching its destination.

41

4. Decide if you have a back-up player who could be used in an emergency.

As you take up your position decide on at least two players who should be in a position to receive your pass. As the whistle goes or play is called react quickly, as the quicker throw is always of advantage to the team in possession; any delay allows the defending team time to sum up and react to the situation and it adds to your pressure as the three seconds tick away.

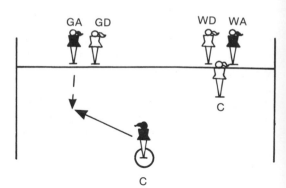

Fig 62   Use the easier pass to the GA.

EARLY PRACTICES
1.   Begin with three players: a thrower, a receiver and a defender. The defender takes up different positions; the thrower has to decide where to throw depending on the receiver's position and what type of throw will be most successful.
2.   Use four players: a thrower, two receivers and a defender. The defender makes the decision to mark one of the receivers and the thrower makes the decision to throw to an unmarked player.
3.   Use six players at a centre pass: three attackers and three defenders. The centre throws from the centre circle and therefore makes the decision as to who is in the most favourable position to receive and makes the correct selection of pass. The defending centre should change her position in order to create different problems for the thrower, as illustrated in Figs 62 to 64.

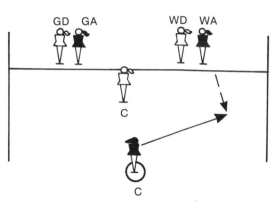

Fig 63   Now the WA is available.

MORE ADVANCED PRACTICES
1.   Use six players at a throw-in: three attackers and three defenders. The player taking the throw-in has to make the decisions that the centre had to make in Exercise 3 of the previous section.
2.   Again use six players but close to the

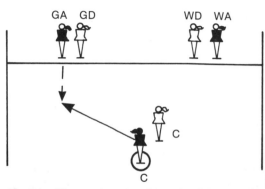

Fig 64   The easier pass is to the GA.

attacking circle when there is a penalty against a defending circle player outside the circle. The wing attack must choose the most favourable player and make the correct choice of throw.

3. Use five players in and around the attacking circle for a free pass to be taken by the attacking team. One of the shooters positions herself to protect a space. The thrower must attempt to put the ball into this protected space rather than give the more dangerous pass to her other shooter (*see* Fig 65). Use good footwork and make the correct choice of throw.

SHOOTING

Shooting is a vitally important skill to learn, as games are won by the scoring of goals from within the goal-circle. It is one of the relatively few 'closed' skills and therefore can be practised at an early stage in total isolation from other game skills. To maintain accuracy the player must develop a technique and rhythm which is safe and solid. In this way she will be able to withstand pressures within the game from opponents who will be doing their best to try to make her change her rhythm and alter her delivery. The rules of the game limit the distance that the defender can be from the shooter and it is therefore in her interest to develop an action which will maintain this advantage. As the protected distance is measured from the landing foot of the player in possession, the shooting action should be learned with this foot being the nearer foot to the post and therefore the defender. Soon she will need to learn to step forwards, backwards or to the side in order to take advantage of the situation within the game, but she must be safe

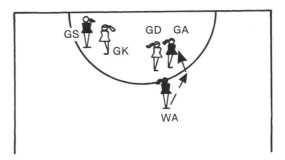

Fig 65   The GA is holding good space. Try a bounce or a drop pass.

and secure within the basic shot before she progresses to stepping and shooting (*see* page 45).

The Static Shot *(Figs 66–9)*

The shooter should take up a comfortable stance close to the post with one foot in front of the other with her body-weight mainly over her rear foot. Her leading foot should ideally be the landing foot but she should practise with either foot leading, so that she can cope with either situation in a game. Her rear leg should be bent slightly, the ball being held as high as possible and balanced on her shooting hand with her fingers spread and pointing backwards with her wrist relaxed. The shooting action is generated from the knees, up through the hips, the shoulders and the arms. The ball is finally released from above the head with a flick of her wrist and fingers. During this action the body-weight is transferred forwards on to her leading foot and her hands follow-through, her shooting hand staying with the ball for as long as possible. The actual flight of the ball will be dependent upon the distance from the post, but a higher trajectory will produce a cleaner entrance into the ring as seen in Fig 69, and should be encouraged.

43

Unfortunately in the British Isles most netball is played outdoors and shooters tend to develop a flatter shot which is less affected by weather conditions. However, it does mean that the entry to the ring becomes more restricted and greater accuracy is required. Throughout the shooting action the head should be held still and the eyes fixed on the ring. The shooter should aim to give enough impetus to the ball to enable it to clear the front rim easily and enter cleanly through the ring or via the middle of the back part of the ring. In netball, only two players on each team, the goal shooter and goal attack, are allowed to attempt shots and therefore their accuracy decides the

Fig 67   Wrist and fingers direct the ball towards the target.

Figs 66 & 67   Relaxed wrist with weight on the back foot.

Fig 68   The flat trajectory which is to be discouraged.

Fig 69   The high trajectory which is
more successful.

Figs 70 & 71   Stepping forward but
maintaining a balanced position.

outcome of the game. Much pressure is
heaped on their shoulders and they must
learn to take this if they are to be members of a winning team.

Stepping and Shooting *(Figs 70–2)*

There are times in a game when it is to
the advantage of the shooter to step
before shooting:

(i)   her view of the post may be
obscured by the hand of a tall defender;
(ii)   the defender may have mistimed her
jump and the shooter may wish to step
round her in order to get closer to the post;
(iii)   the shooter may have gained possession directly under the ring and may
have to step back to gain a more accessible shooting position;
(iv)   the defender may have been penal-
ized and the shooter may use the opportunity to step away from her in order to get
a closer shot and to be in a better position
to rebound the attempted shot.
    In all these cases the shooter should
begin as if she is going to attempt a static shot and the target should have her
total concentration as she steps either

Fig 71   Raise the knee to begin the
upward thrust.

forwards, to the side or backwards. The stepping foot must not be the landing foot as this would break the footwork rule. As her weight is transferred to her stepping foot, the landing foot is lifted and her knee raised to help to maintain a balanced position. This balance is important if the rhythm of the static shot is to be reproduced. The upward thrust is initiated by the weight of the transference from the heel to the ball of the foot, up through the extension of the knee and onward through the body as in the static shot. The shot should be practised stepping forwards, to the side and backwards, always trying to maintain a balanced shot from the stepping foot.

Jumping and Shooting (Fig 73)

The same shooting action should be tried beginning with a jump, rather than a step forward from the landing foot. This can be an additional skill and is useful if the shooter needs to move further away from an opponent at a penalty shot or when receiving a pass on the move with a clear run to the post. Again the rhythm should be maintained with the landing, jump, balance and shot all completed in a smooth and controlled manner. This

Fig 72 Joan Bryan (Birmingham) steps back to gain a better position.

Fig 73 The GS steps away from her opponent and prepares to jump and shoot.

can be developed to include another jump as the shot is made, but this is a very advanced skill and should only be practised when the basic skill of shooting is very well established.

Off-balance Shooting *(Fig 74)*

Quite often during a game the shooter may find herself falling out of court when by the post. It is useful to practise shooting whilst falling as the ability to achieve the balanced shooting position whilst in the air soon becomes a very useful skill and can be very rewarding, delighting the spectators as well as the performer when successful.

Fig 74   Try to retain balance to shoot whilst falling.

1. Practise the static shot from a position close to the post. Concentrate on using the correct technique and try to develop a shooting rhythm. If you are inaccurate, find out where you are inaccurate – is it in direction, distance or height? Try to correct the fault by attending to the detail and repeat the action until you score ten times from the same spot, only then move to another spot.

2. Mark the goal-circle with twelve chalk crosses randomly spaced at various distances from the goal-post. Then carry out the following:

(a) practise the static shot from each position only moving on to the next cross when five goals have been scored;

(b) repeat (a) but on each occasion step either forward, to the side or backwards trying to improve your balance and technique during each shot;

(c) repeat (a) but try to keep concentrating on your balance and achieving good technique, whilst a defender attempts to intercept a shot.

3. Work with a partner, with you beginning as the shooter and your partner as the feeder. Start outside the goal-circle and pass the ball to your partner at the front of the circle and receive a return pass as you run into the circle towards the post. Catch the ball and try to land facing the goal-post. Aim for a balanced, controlled landing and shot at goal. Each time you should make a note of your landing foot and aim always to shoot with this foot forward.

4. Work with your partner again, this time beginning your practice from a position under the post. Your partner stands on the edge of the circle holding the ball.

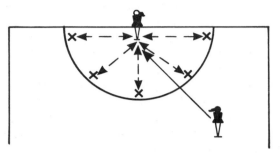

Fig 75 Watch the feeder at all times.

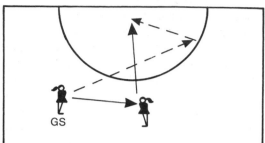

Fig 76 Aim for a smooth change of direction.

Run out to touch the circle edge and return to receive a pass near the post. Return the ball to your feeder and repeat the movement three times before shooting for goal. Always aim for perfect balance, rhythm and total concentration when shooting. This is a little more difficult when you are breathing heavily; try taking a deep breath just before you shoot to help you to remain calm.

ADVANCED PRACTICES
1. Working with a partner, begin by the post and side-step out to a cross marked on the ground at the edge of the goal-circle and run back in to the post. At all times watch the feeder and change your foot patterns as necessary. The feeder will pass the ball to you as you return towards the post. The feeder begins by passing every time but only passes intermittently;

Summary
The basic skills of netball are catching, throwing and shooting. Young players should learn to:
• catch with one and two hands
• throw with one and two hands and with a variety of types of pass
• shoot with good technique from static and moving situations.

Main Coaching Points
Catching
• watch the ball
• hands should be ball-shaped with fingers spread and angled towards the ball.
• reach out, arms straightening and pull the ball back in to the chest

Throwing
• begin from the catching position with ball held at the chest

• prepare by moving ball to the point where it will be directed forward
• turn body to give balanced throwing position
• step forward and direct the ball towards the target
• follow through to give power and direction

Shooting
• take up a comfortable stance with feet slightly apart for balance
• hold the ball high on fingers of favoured hand
• use second hand on the side of the ball for support
• look and concentrate on a point above the ring
• push up beginning at the knees and ending with the fingers
• follow through

you should shoot whenever you receive a pass. If the pass does not come, move on to the next cross. (*See* Fig 75.)

2. Again in pairs, move around some cones placed randomly in the circle and then make a definite move towards the post. The feeder, from a position just outside the circle, sees the move and passes you the ball. You should catch the ball, control your movement, balance and shoot. Return the ball to the feeder and repeat the activity. If the feeder does not give you a pass, move around the cones again and make a more determined effort. It is important to keep eye contact with the feeder at all times.

3. Working with a partner, begin outside the circle (*see* Fig 76). Pass the ball to your partner and then run across the circle edge and take a pass as you head towards the post. Catch in the air, land, step and make a shot. Aim for the whole movement to be smooth with quick concentration on the target as soon as the ball is in your hands.

4 Movement Skills

Netball is basically a throwing and catching game played on the move. Although many of the skills are best practised statically they are seen at their best when performed on the move in a game situation. The secret of good movement is good footwork. The best players have the ability to sprint, stop, change direction, jump off one or both feet or to run and lunge to take a pass or intercept a pass to an opponent and, at the end of it all, have the control to land and stay within the bounds of the footwork rule. Netball is about movement and when performed well the flow and movement of the game is in no way restricted by the rules governing footwork.

In order to be involved in the game a player must have the ability to move to receive a pass from one of her own players or to be able to intercept a pass from one of her opponents. She must be able to attack or defend whenever necessary.

ATTACKING

A player needs to constantly try to make herself available to receive a pass. If she is not used, she needs to be able to make herself available for the next pass and the next, if necessary. This is called 'getting free', of which there are many methods. Some players have a favourite method but the best players resort to a variety of methods and are able to select the appropriate one according to their opponents and the type of game being played.

Methods of Getting Free

SPRINTING
When a player is being closely marked she can suddenly sprint into an open and clear area of the court. The ideal situation is if she sprints away from the side her opponent is covering – the unmarked side – and also moves to catch the ball at the position where her path and the path of the thrown ball would meet at a right angle as illustrated in Fig 77.

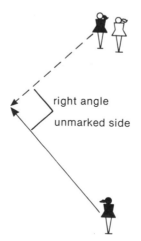

right angle

unmarked side

Fig 77   Sprinting away to the unmarked side.

This is the ideal manoeuvre and as such should be a starting point for beginners. In a game situation this is not always possible and the player will choose the direction according to her position in relation to the thrower and her opponent.

50

PREPARATORY MOVEMENT AND SPRINT

The player may make some type of movement first in order to confuse or unbalance her opponent and then sprint off in the opposite direction, into the space. This is commonly called 'dodging' and the movements may take the form of:

(i)   one, two or even more, short, sharp movements from side to side with the top half of your body, keeping your feet still, before sprinting off in a more favourable direction. This is called a feint dodge as shown in Figs 78 to 80.

(ii)   a strong movement to one side stepping on your outside foot, pulling back and sprinting off in the opposite direction. The final step may be preceded by one or two small foot movements. (*See* Figs 81 to 83.)

(iii)   a strong step across your body with the foot nearest to your opponent. Then pivot on this foot turning away from and turning your back on your opponent, who hopefully has committed herself to the first direction, then sprint off into the space that has opened up in front or to the opposite side. This is called the reverse pivot and is illustrated by Figs 84 to 86.

All these preparatory movements need to be performed suddenly and sharply or else your opponent will not be put off and beaten.

SPRINTING AND FOLLOWING ACTION

You may find that neither the sprint nor any of the dodges have shaken off your

Figs 78–80 Top half moves one way, then quickly to the other side prior to sprinting away before the opponent has recovered.

Fig 79.

Fig 80.

Figs 81–3   A strong step to the right
taking the opponent with you, then
quickly changing to the other side and
sprinting away.

Fig 82.

Fig 83.

opposition and whilst sprinting hard your opponent is still too close for comfort, in which case you may resort to:

(i) suddenly stopping and allowing your opponent to carry on and either stepping or sprinting in the opposite direction to take the pass. This is a change of direction method;

(ii) suddenly stopping and as your opponent slows down, suddenly sprinting on again in the same direction. This is a run, stop, run method;

(iii) suddenly bending and turning away by rolling and turning your back on your opponent and the player with the ball. Quickly turn to regain eye contact with your thrower and sprint off in the opposite direction. This is called rolling off and it frees you to take the pass or the one after, if so desired. (*See* Figs 87 and 88.)

Figs 84–6   The reverse pivot – use the foot nearest to the opponent in order to commit her.

Fig 85   Pivot on that foot turning away from the opponent.

Fig 86   Sprint off into the space on the opposite side.

Figs 87 & 88   Turn away from the opponent by rolling onwards.

Fig 88   Sprint into space on the opposite side to receive the pass.

Figs 89 & 90 Facing your opponent to protect a space.

Fig 90 Quickly turn to receive a pass.

PROTECTING A SPACE *(Figs 89–92)*
The player may find that she can control the movement of her opponent by using her own body as a barrier. In this way she can prevent her from moving into the area where she wishes to catch the ball – this is called protecting a space. She may be protecting a space that she can run into or it may be a space close to her that she can step or reach into. She may protect the space by facing her opponent and then turning into the space or by placing her back to her opponent and then stepping away from her into the protected space. In all cases communication between the attacker and the thrower is vital so that the ball is directed into the protected space, either close enough to be reached or far enough ahead to be caught on the run.

Communication between thrower and catcher may be made through the use of the body, the eyes or the hands and the player must learn to spot the 'cues' in

Figs 91 & 92 Holding a strong position with your back to your opponent.

Fig 92   Step into the protected space.

order to deliver the right type of pass, at the right moment. The attacker must be firm and strong in her movements and must be definite and positive in where and when she wants the ball. Any hesitation will allow the defender to catch up and so take away the attacker's initiative.

EARLY PRACTICES

1. The basic methods of making oneself available can be practised in isolation and without the ball to begin with. This overlaps with the earlier footwork practices but very quickly the ball should be added. The ability to read cues, as to when and where to move in relation to the thrower and the thrower's ability to release the ball should be learned through simple practices with three players; a feeder, a defender and a player trying to get free, in these ways:

(a) sprint away from the defender to receive a pass;
(b) feint in one direction but quickly sprint off in another direction to receive the pass;
(c) sprint away from the defender and if she is still close to you, suddenly stop and sprint back towards your starting position to receive the pass.

2. Add a fourth player to pass the ball to the thrower, this will help the attacker make her attempt to get free at the right time. She should wait for eye contact before making her move.

3. Use six players, four attackers and two defenders as in Fig 93. Begin with the first attacker, who passes the ball to her first team-mate to move to make herself available. She then passes the ball on to her team-mate who times her move and then passes on to the final attacker. The

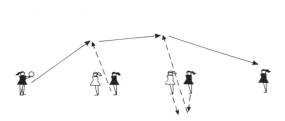

Fig 93   Time your move using a variety of methods of getting free.

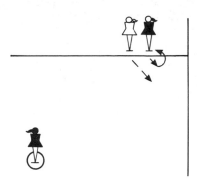

Figs 94 & 95   Reverse pivot at the centre pass – step into the centre court using your right leg.

move can then be reversed.
4. To practise getting free at a centre pass, work in threes and explore the use of the previous methods.

MORE ADVANCED PRACTICES
1. The difficult techniques involved in becoming available by using reverse pivot, holding and protecting space and rolling off need to be practised in isolation. Initially practise the following without a ball and then progress to having a thrower feeding the ball into the right space:

(a) reverse pivot and its use at a centre pass (see Figs 94 and 95);
(b) protecting space and moving into space at a throw in;
(c) protecting space and stepping and turning into space;
(d) rolling off and creating alternative space, shown previously in Figs 87 and 88.

2. It is important to use as many methods of getting free and to make as many offers to receive the ball as possible:

(a) first use a thrower T and attacker A who receives the ball four times using a different method of getting free from an imaginary defender, each time (see Fig 96);

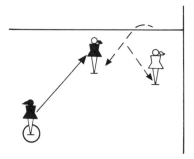

Fig 95   Pivot and sprint into the centre court on the opposite side of your opponent.

Fig 96   Make a different move each time.

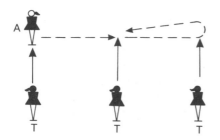

Fig 97   Can you work under pressure?

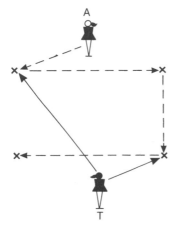

Fig 98   Offer to take the ball at each cross.

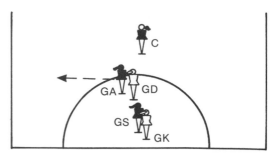

Figs 99 & 100   The GA can clear a space for the GS.

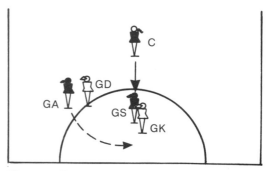

Fig 100   The GA then makes a second move.

(b) repeat Practice (a) but the thrower only passes the ball when she wants to. If the attacker offers to receive the ball and is not given it then she must offer somewhere else and even again if necessary; (c) now add a defender and try again with the thrower only passing when her attacker is free.

3. Use two or even three throwers, each with a ball keeping the pressure on the attacker who must offer to receive from any of the throwers who may or may not pass the ball. The attacker should display a wide range of methods of getting free. (*See* Fig 97.) Continue by adding a defender.

4. Use one thrower T and an attacker A as in Fig 98, the attacker must make a move to receive the ball at each cross. The thrower does not have to pass.
5. A clearing move in the circle. (*See* Figs 99 and 100.) If the move to get free is performed well the opponent will be drawn out with the move. In a team situation this can be used to advantage in that it clears a space for another member of the team to move into as shown in Fig 101. The original player can then make another move to take the ball later.

Remember when learning the attacking moves, timing is very important. If you make your move too soon your opponent catches you up, if you start creeping towards your space your opponent

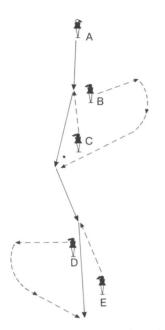

Fig 101   Make your move to clear the space.

begins to creep also. Use your eyes, be positive and you should be successful.

DEFENDING

A defending move is any move made by opponents which is aimed at checking the progress of the team in possession of the ball. Success is measured in many different ways:

(i)   a player is marked so closely that she is unable to receive the ball;
(ii)   the defending player is able to intercept a pass meant for the attacking team;
(iii) the attacking player is deprived of the opportunity of entering the area which will give her most advantage;
(iv)   the defending player is able to pressurize the player in possession of the ball to such an extent that possession is lost.

The best defenders have good footwork and handling skills, are agile and alert enough to read and anticipate the moves of their opponents. Although specific positions within the team indicate the defensive nature of their role, such as goalkeeper, goal defence or wing defence, it is still very important that all players in a team become defenders when possession of the ball has been lost. In order to regain possession every throw and catch must be made whilst under intense pressure from defenders. It is this pressure that finally results in the attackers making a hurried or rash pass or causes mishandling on the part of the catcher. If this breakdown can be made early in the passage of the ball down the court, then there is a greater chance of a goal being scored – an interception by the goal shooter gives her team an instant scoring opportunity and therefore is even more valuable.

There are many ways of defending but the basic method is when each player within the team makes it her job to defend her own opponent. This is known as 'man-to-man' defending and is the normal starting point when learning the skills of defending. This means that all players should be able to perform the majority of defending skills, although some players may require extra, more specific skills relevant to their playing positions such as defending the shot or rebounding missed shots. All players must therefore practise the main defending skills.

Marking (Figs 102–6)

This involves taking up a position so close to an opponent that a pass to her would be risky and if made could easily be intercepted by the marking defender.

Fig 102   The basic front marking position.

Fig 103   Turning in to mark from the side.

The defender should stand slightly in front of her opponent and in such a position that her right shoulder is level with and covering the left shoulder of her opponent. From this position the defender can watch both her opponent and the thrower. The footbase of the defender should be reasonably compact and the knees slightly bent. From this position she can shadow the movements of her opponent and yet can still react by jumping upwards or stretching sidewards if the ball is thrown. Defenders need to maintain constant and intense concentration, though due to the rules of the game the thrower must release the ball within a time limit of three seconds and therefore the concentrated effort is only for a short span of time. It can also be a very rewarding effort if done well. The wise defender knows her own ability and

can even drop off from her opponent just enough to encourage the pass and then move back to make a timely interception.

The basic marking position may be varied according to where the pass is coming from or the type of game. If the ball is coming from the front, use the normal marking position – in front and slightly to the side covering half of the opponent's body. If the ball is coming from the side, adjust your foot position turning more towards the opponent, taking up a more sideways position or even turning inwards to slightly face her. Keep an eye on the ball by watching over your shoulder. This allows easier side-stepping movements towards the catcher if she should choose to drop back for an overhead pass.

If you wish to prevent the attacker from coming forward, take up a position facing your opponent totally. Concentrate on

Fig 104   Prevent your opponent from moving down the court.

Fig 105   Force your opponent to move forward.

her, shadowing her movements and preventing her from getting past into a forward space. However, this is a negative method of defending as you are unlikely to be able to intercept the ball but it can be a useful ploy if you have found that your opponent has constantly got the better of you and is a very influential member of the attacking team. Taking her out of the game, even for a short span of time, may disrupt the play of your opponents causing them to make mistakes, which gives possession to your team.

If you wish to force the attacker to go forward, take up a position behind her to deny her the opportunity to move backwards. This again reduces your opportunity to intercept but it may be useful in forcing one of the shooters to move further away from the post and to make her attempt a longer shot. If she is very tall

Fig 106   Colette Thompson (England) shows good concentration when marking back.

and has been able to receive a high over-head ball without you being able to do anything about it, then it may be useful for you to try this different ploy. It may even force her out of the circle which has to be to your advantage.

When defending you will find yourself moving from one marking method to another according to the flow and pattern of the game. You will require agility of body and footwork in order to cope with the constant adjustment of position. This will allow you to keep a tight pressure on your opponent in order to give your own team the advantage. Remember that the team rules governing marking are:

(i) there must be no contact body, arms, hands or knees;
(ii) the arms must remain close to the body at all times being used solely for normal body balance – drifting sideways or around opponents is not allowed.

Remember that the three seconds rule is always in the defender's favour and pro-viding you can concentrate for that length of time you will exert pressure on not only your own opponent who, in her frustration, may ask for the pass, but also on the thrower who is aware that time is running out and she must release the ball. The interception which should result is the reward for all your effort.

Intercepting

In most cases intercepting is caused by good, close marking. Hard defending down the court by all members of the team may eventually cause the loose pass or indecision in the attacker in her efforts to get free from her tightly marking oppon-ent. The player making the interception

will get all the glory but will admit the part played by her team-mates. The clean inter-ception from in front of the opponent is the ideal but the tip or bat to another mem-ber of your team is of equal value, as is the deflection out of court which gives your team time to reposition. The interception, as well as being made from in front can be made from behind, but in all cases agility, footwork, good handling and, above all, a sense of timing are prime requisites. The ability to remain concentrated and alert, to be able to sense when the attacker is mak-ing her final move to receive the pass and at that moment being able to be totally committed to cutting off the ball *en route* to the catcher, are all essential elements of good defending and are what make inter-ceptions possible. It is this close marking and continual attempts at interception of the ball which make up the first stage of defending.

Being aware of your own ability and knowing the interceptions which are with-in your scope and therefore worth attempting are also valued qualities of the defender. The player who arrives too late for an interception or who takes a superb interception and lands on her opponent is more of a liability than an asset. One expects beginner players to go all out for the interceptions knowing that some-times they will get it wrong, but as they get more experienced they will be expect-ed to be able to make the correct decision as to whether they can make a valid con-tribution by going for the interception. Practice and greater agility ensure a greater range of intercepting qualities.

INTERCEPTING FROM THE FRONT *(Fig 107)*
Take up a close marking position in front of your opponent and shadow her move-ments. Notice when she begins to make

Fig 107   Jesslyn Parkes (England) shows a good extended interception.

Fig 108   Lorna Hylton (England under-21) shows good technique when making a clean overhead interception of the lob pass.

her final commitment – her stride will lengthen and her body will lean in the direction of the final run. As soon as you spot this, turn your attention away from the marked player and give total concentration to the ball. Lengthen your own stride and thrust off to attempt to take the ball cleanly in front of your opponent. It is of advantage to attempt to cut across the angle as this makes interceptions easier and also helps to avoid any body contact.

If possible try to take the interception with both hands, but it may be necessary to take with one hand only to gain that extra reach. If using just one hand, immediately try to bring the ball quickly into the safety of two hands. If neither of these are possible try to bat or knock the ball into the space ahead and chase after it to claim possession. Remember, in all cases, to control your feet on landing and prepare to make a pass to one of your teammates. This is the time to take a little extra time to allow your own players to readjust to the changing circumstances. It is the moment when so many rash passes are made and the advantage of the interception is lost – so take that little extra time. If you fail to make contact with the ball, recover quickly and try to get back between your opponent and the goal.

When intercepting in front of a static player, the lob over the head to the standing player may cause you to move backwards to attempt the interception. In this situation good footwork is important in order to move close enough to the player to be in a position to make an upward jump to attempt to intercept the ball without making contact with the player. This is helped if the landing is made on the foot nearest the player and then the ball and your body-weight are pulled back towards the direction of the thrower.

Figs 109 & 110   Intercepting from behind the opponent – weight moves to the outside leg.

Fig 110   Thrust from the outside leg to attack the line of flight of the ball.

INTERCEPTING FROM BEHIND
(Figs 109 & 110)
There are times in the game when it is an advantage to defend from a position behind the attacker. Having committed yourself to defending in this manner, you should have the skill and ability to move round to attempt an interception if the ball is in the air for any length of time. It

is possible if you are alert and use good footwork. There are two ways of tackling this problem:
(i)   assess when the pass is to be made and make a quick step to the side and slightly forward of the catcher. Then bring your nearer leg through and forward in front avoiding any contact. Step forward on to that foot as you attack the line of flight of the ball in order to make the interception;
(ii)   assess when the pass is to be made and make a quick step round the catcher using your foot which is the furthest away from her. Bring your far hand and shoulder round and across and from a position almost facing her, deflect the ball away. Your hand is turned away from the catcher and is commonly called 'reverse handling'. Chase and recover the ball.

This is a very useful answer to an underarm, a bounce or drop pass when the normal interception would not be possible without contact being made. If all efforts at first stage defending fail and the opponent manages to catch the ball, then the defender's job changes and she moves into the second stage of defending – that of defending the player in possession of the ball.

Defending the Player with the Ball

The rules state that a player in possession of the ball can be defended by an opponent provided that the opponent is at least 0.9m (3ft) away from the player's original landing foot. The opponent can attempt to do this by:

(i) staying on the ground with her arms spread out and forward, trying to cover the possible path of the ball as it is thrown (*see* Fig 111). She can use one or two

64

Fig 111   Stay on the ground and try to cover the ball.

hands and hopefully cause the thrower to adapt her throw to avoid the hands. This may result in a more loopy type of throw which will make an interception further down the court a greater possibility.

(ii) Jumping forwards and upwards to try to anticipate the path and timing of the throw in order to make an interception or to deflect the ball as in Fig 112. This is quite difficult to do and requires much practice. A mistimed jump also gives the immediate advantage to the attacking player, as she can then step round the defender to give the pass and is then free to be further involved in the play if needed.

The recovery from marking, or from a missed interception into defending from a position in front of the player, requires quick footwork and balance. It is a skill that requires much practice in order to avoid infringing the defending distance

Fig 112   Jump to try and anticipate the release and flight of the ball.

rule, 0.9m (3ft). A penalty pass or shot is not going to help you as it deprives your team of a player, as the offending player must stand at the side of the thrower and not move until the ball has left the thrower's hands. It is therefore worth putting in the practice in order to get this right.

Defending the Player without the Ball

If your efforts at defending the player with the ball fail and the ball has passed you then it is time to move into the third stage of defending. Here you need to try to keep your opponent from being further involved in the play and for as long as possible by continually depriving her of forward space. If you can 'face mark' the thrower after she has released the ball you can delay her progress down the court and prevent her from being further involved in the attack. This is a good tactic when performed safely but remember that your hands must stay close to your body and your knees must not be used to prevent your opponent from passing you – remember that a penalty pass or shot against you will not help your own team. Delay her by using quick, short steps to form a block on her passage down the court.

If the attacker manages to pass you then turn and run alongside her ready to mark or attempt an interception if she moves for another pass. The same movement can be used to prevent the goal shooter from getting back into the circle if she has been brave enough to leave it to take the pass.

Remember that however you choose to defend you must stay within the rules of the game. The umpire will soon let you know whether she agrees with you or not and you must adjust your game to con-

form with the interpretations made by the umpire. A silly penalty against a defender, particularly if it is within the shooting circle, could result in a goal-scoring attempt for the opposition – so stay disciplined and in control.

Defending a Shot at Goal
(Figs 113–15)

This is similar to the second stage of defending, but in this case the player with the ball has a fixed and clearly defined target – the goal-ring and when defending your movements can therefore be more concentrated. As it is only the goal-keeper and goal defence who can defend the shot from within the goal circle they require a specialist skill. The shot can only be defended with a distance of 0.9m (3ft) between the landing foot of the shooter and your nearest foot. The shot can be defended from in front, at the side or from the rear, but normally you will take up your position between the shooter and the goal-post. From this position you can put pressure on the shooter in several ways:

(i) you can take the weight on to your front foot and reach upwards and forwards with one arm to try to cover the flight the ball will take towards the goal-post. Your back foot can be raised in order to reach closer to the ball's path and the position should be held for three seconds or until after the ball is released; (ii) you can stand on both feet and raise both hands forwards and upwards to cover the expected flight path of the shot. This position has the advantage that you can move and adapt easily if the shooter decides to make a pass instead of a shot; (iii) you can stand at the correct

Fig 113   Sharron Burridge (New Zealand) shows perfect balance when defending the shot.

distance, bend your knees and jump forwards and upwards, stretching one hand up as far as possible in order to intercept or deflect the ball on its flight path towards the goal-ring. The timing of this jump is critical; jump too soon and the shooter will wait, step forward and around you getting a closer shot and being in a good position to catch or tip the ball on the rebound if the shot is missed – 'rebounding'. If you jump too late, the ball will have passed the critical point where contact was possible. Ideally your jump should be performed during the downward movement of the shooter so you are at the full height of the jump as the shooter releases the ball upwards. Be careful as so often the jump is made as the shooter pushes upwards when it is too late.

Remember that you must not touch the ball whilst it is still in the hands of the

Fig 114   Gill Davies (England) raises both hands to cover the expected flight path of the shot.

Fig 115 The GD jumps to put the shooter under pressure.

the outer area of the circle. Failure, however, puts you out of the game until you can regain your balance and distance; you have little chance of challenging for the rebound from a missed shot. You should make a choice of method depending on the shooter's stature and your own, the shooter's shooting style and your own skill and ability.

Rebounding the Missed Shot

Both defenders have a job to do and they should attempt to work as a pair to reduce the opportunities of the shooting team.

DEFENDING THE SHOOTER MAKING THE SHOT (Figs 116 & 117)

As soon as the ball has been released you should turn your back on the shooter in order to prevent her from moving forward. At the same time watch for the flight of the ball and make a strong upward jump to take any rebound from the post which comes into your area. It is safer to attempt to take with both hands but a

shooter, nor must you touch any part of the arm or hand of the shooter. If you do a penalty pass or shot will be awarded against you and that is always going to give a greater advantage to the shooter. If, however, the shooter steps forward reducing the distance you are allowed to continue with your normal defending, which will give you the advantage. If you both move forward and collide, the umpire will probably give a toss-up between you as both of you are at fault.

Using method (i) or (ii) means you are less likely to be able to intercept the ball but you are in a good position to turn after the ball has been released and are strongly placed to rebound a missed shot. The third method gives a better chance of interception, particularly if you are tall and the shot is being taken from

Figs 116 & 117 Make a quick turn after the shot has been made.

Fig 117　Rebound strongly to gain good possession from a missed shot.

Figs 118–20　GD takes up a wide firm stance under the post.

Fig 119　Jump firmly to block out your opponent and take the rebound.

Fig 120　GD prepares to start her team on to the attack.

higher reach can be made with one hand and the ball pulled back into two hands or batted or tipped away into a safer catching position. Be strong and firm throughout and have a wide landing base. When successful keep the ball safe and close to the body whilst you make the decision on how to begin your team's attack.

DEFENDING THE SHOOTER WITHOUT POSSESSION UNDER THE POST
(Figs 118–20)
Take up a firm, wide stance under the post and between your opponent and the shooter in possession. Have your knees slightly flexed and ready for movement with your whole body and arms in a state of alertness. Remember that the other shooter may decide to pass rather than shoot. If the ball rebounds off the post, jump firmly upwards blocking out the movement of the other shooter towards the ball, take the ball cleanly and land firm, wide and balanced ready to start the next attack.

Do not fight for possession with your own defender; with a good understanding you can make a formidable pair. Be dominant over your opponents by getting to the more desirable space first. Do not allow them to dictate to you; be the master of your own area and then you will be successful.

Early Practices

Defending the shot and rebounding are specific skills which must be practised in isolation. They require good technique and until this is acquired a greater awareness of the whole circle area is unlikely to be achieved. Spend time acquiring these skills and find out where your strengths are. Are you better at holding or do you have good elevation and timing? Spend time now to make yourself a better player and you are sure to make a valuable contribution to the team.

More Advanced Practices

1. In pairs, one shooter and one defender; the defender covers the shot at goal by leaning. As the ball is released, the defender turns towards the post and blocks off the shooter's movement towards the post by taking up a strong wide stance. Then she should aim to step forward and jump to take the rebound if it is a missed shot.
2. Again in pairs, one shooter and one defender; the shooter steps forward or to the side in order to avoid the defender. The defender moves to cover the shot but is careful to maintain the original 0.9m (3ft) distance. She should not give way to the shooter's forward movement; it is she who is reducing the distance and the umpire will be aware of that. Add another

Fig 121   GK stays strong when GS steps forward and reduces the distance.

pair as a shooter and defender who compete under the goal-post for the rebound from any missed shots. (*See* Fig 121.)
3. Now in threes, an attacker feeding in to her shooter and a defender; the defender close-marks the shooter and if she fails to prevent her from getting the ball, she quickly moves round and into a position to defend the shot. She should be careful to pull her hand back into her body until the correct position is achieved and then raise it to cover the shot.

Remember, however you chose to defend, know your own strengths and try to make use of them. If you can hang back and yet have the speed to come in for a late interception then make use of this. If your strength is the hounding of your opponent by close-marking to prevent her from getting into the game then resort to this method. But remember that within a team situation you may be asked to use a specific method which the coach feels will upset the opposition and will bring a greater success to your team. You should therefore work on your weaknesses and learn to become equally capable at all methods – then you really will be an asset to your team.

Summary

All players must have the ability to move into a space to receive a pass, and to move to intercept a pass intended for another player. Earlier footwork and ball skills should give the players the means to get free from an opponent and also to stay close to an opponent. These skills form the basis of good attacking and defending play.

Attacking Skills

Players should develop a variety of methods of getting away from an opponent and should be able to select the best method according to the situation. Methods include:

- sprinting
- sprinting and stopping
- dodging
- changing direction
- protecting space.

Defending Skills

Defending skills are used to prevent the team in possession from making progress towards their shooting end. Skills include:

- close man-to-man marking
- intercepting
- marking in front of the player with the ball
- delaying the forward movement of the player after she has thrown the ball.

It is important to be able to move from one method to another according to the situation.

Circle defenders should practise defending the shot by leaning, holding a position or jumping, and should be encouraged to select according to the situation

Circle defenders should also practise rebounding after defending the shot and also rebounding missed shots from standing positions under the post.

5 Playing a Position

It is useful when learning to play the game of netball for all young players to sample each position. Every position is different – each has general skills but there are also more specific skills. By playing each position the young player will get an idea of the individual requirements and will eventually settle down to playing any of two or three positions well. The lucky ones who are chosen to play for their country will have become specialists in one position but will also be able to play another position as a second choice.

If they find they are strong on defending they will probably choose to play one of the three defending positions, wing defence (WD), goal defence (GD) or goal-keeper (GK). If they are better at attacking they will settle for the attacking positions of centre (C), wing attack (WA) or goal attack (GA). If their strength is in shooting accurately then they will favour goal attack (GA) or goal shooter (GS).

It may be that their stature helps them to choose; the tall players tend to favour either end of the court and the shorter players the central positions. Whatever position they have chosen they will be part of a team and it is when all the players' skills merge to produce a good team performance that life gets difficult for the opponents. This chapter will look at each position in turn and will try to point out any specialist needs, as well as giving hints and tips on how to play the position well.

GOAL SHOOTER

The main need of the goal shooter is the specialist ability to shoot accurately and so score goals. This requires confidence, balance, strength and concentration. Yet all of this is to no avail if the player is unable to receive the ball within the circle area. For this reason, height is a great asset as it allows the shooter to take a high pass and to retrieve rebounds under the post. It is, however, not a necessity and a more mobile player with good skills and elevation will probably perform equally as well, if not better than the taller but perhaps less mobile player. A goal shooter also requires judgement in assessing when to stay in a strong holding position under the post and when to move out in order to take the pass herself or in order to clear a space for her goal attack. However she plays the game, she will be a major deciding factor as to whether her team wins or loses and she must be able to cope with the pressure that this entails.

Hints and Tips

1. Take up a position within the shooting circle from which you can make a variety of movements. Try dodges, sprints, dropping back, lunging forward, turning, pivoting and rolling off. Wherever your opponent stands you should have some options open to you. Practise with a feeder only and then add a defender. (*See* Fig 122.)
2. Be prepared to leave the circle to

Fig 122   GS shows clearly where she wants the ball. The back foot is kept firmly down to give her a closer shot.

receive a pass, but when you do, sprint out forcefully, hopefully pulling your opponent with you to create more space for your goal attack.

3. Develop the skill to work your way back into the circle – this requires good footwork and good attacking skills. Use two of your court players to help you to pass a defending player and return into the circle. When you get there, either shoot for goal or use the court players to work your way closer to the post. Always be prepared to rebound any missed shots.

4. Be prepared to take up a firm stance and hold your position strongly until you are able to turn and lunge towards your team-mate with the ball. Keep your

back foot down and as close to the post as possible.

5. Practise at least one hundred shots each day. Mark points on the ground and do five shots before moving on to the next point. Practise stepping forwards, stepping to the side and stepping backwards. Be accurate and be prepared to rebound strongly if the shot fails to score.

6. You must work with your goal attack and be able to play her position. Work with her at creating space for each other. You may not even get the ball but you will have taken your opponent away and made it easier to get closer to the post. (See Figs 123 & 124.)

7. Give clear information to your teammates as to where and when you want the ball delivered to you. Always discuss any breakdown in communications and get it right the next time.

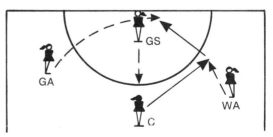

Figs 123 & 124   GS creates space by moving forward, and by making a strong move out to one side.

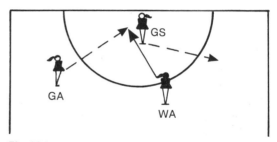

Fig 124.

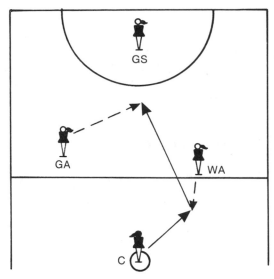

Figs 125 & 126 GA makes her move for the second pass.

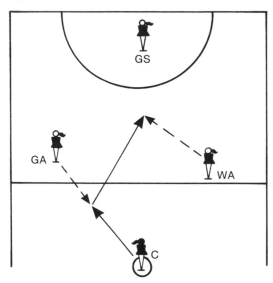

Fig 126 Here she interchanges with the WA and takes the first pass.

8. You should be prepared to defend as far as the third line when your team has lost possession – an interception by you is worth two by your defenders.

GOAL ATTACK

Speed, mobility and the ability to shoot accurately are the prime skills of this position. Add to these the abilities to take a good pass and to be able to feed the shooter using a wide range of throws and you have a very versatile and accomplished player. The ability to move dynamically into the centre court area or into the circle, as well as having the mobility to manoeuvre through crowded areas, makes this the position for a thinking player and someone who can set the game alight. It is also the position where an unthinking and selfish player can undo all the good work of the other members of her team.

Hints and Tips

1. Take up a position, between the transverse line and the edge of the goal-circle, on the opposite side of your WA, where you can drive strongly to the centre court or into the circle, depending on the positioning of your players and your opponents.
2. Practise communicating non-verbally with your wing attack so that you build up an understanding as to who is making the first move as shown in Figs 125 and 126. Develop a good use of space.
3. Develop a variety of passing skills in order to feed the goal shooter according to her position within the circle and that of her opponent. Build up communication until you can read her intentions quickly and respond with the appropriate pass.
4. Be prepared to enter the circle and take over the shooting role if the goal shooter moves out of the circle.
5. Watch your space when entering the circle – work together with the goal

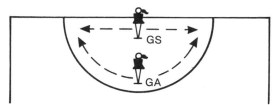

Figs 127–9 Here the split is front and back.

Fig 128 Here each player takes a side.

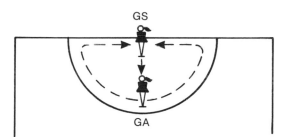

Fig 129 Here the shooters rotate and cause problems for the defenders.

shooter and try different ways of dividing up the circle. (See Figs 127 to 129.)

6. Be prepared to attack strongly into the centre court for a centre pass if needed and be able to pivot and sprint back into the attacking third. Give your wing attack the first choice of position at the centre pass and then position yourself accordingly. Do not take her space by standing too close – be prepared to take the second pass.

7. Practise at least one hundred shots a day. Use crosses on the ground and use your footwork to step forwards, backwards and to the side. Remember to aim

for accuracy from the one cross before progressing to the next.

8. Use your speed and agility to defend in the centre third when your team has lost possession.

WING ATTACK

Speed, mobility and accuracy are essential requirements for a good wing attack. An ability to get free from her opponent in a small space, to be able to receive the centre pass, to possess a wide range of passing skills in order to feed her shooters safely and accurately, are just a few of the skills which any wing attack requires. If you are small, then this could be the position for you, as speed and mobility are more important than stature. The best wing attack will maintain a constant vision of the play as the ball travels down the court. She will take decisions on whether to move strongly forward to get involved in the centre third or whether to hang back and make a move to receive on the circle edge where her accurate skills will be of more use. The player needs excellent communication skills particularly with the shooters and she should be able to respond to the cues which they are giving and make the correct feed into the desired position.

Hints and Tips

1. Take up a position on the opposite side of the court from your goal attack, somewhere between the goal-circle and the transverse line where you are able to move easily in many directions.

2. Form strong links with your goal attack so that you are able to communicate easily and non-verbally.

75

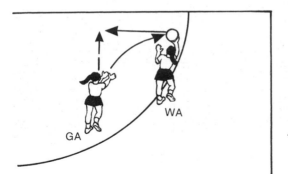

Fig 130   Keep the leg close to the circle upright and strong.

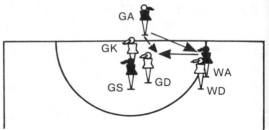

Figs 131 & 132   Here the WA is available for the pass and the quick return.

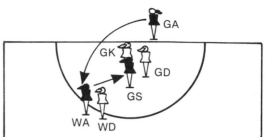

Fig 132   Here she holds a good position to pass to the GS as she turns.

3. Develop a range of passing skills in order to feed the shooters according to their needs and positions. Practise the lob, the chest pass, the drop and bounce pass. Use your footwork to increase your range of delivery and try using the left or the right hand to deliver the pass.

4. Develop the skill of being available around the circle so that either of your shooters can use you in order to work their way closer to the post. Hold a strong position using your foot and leg close to the circle, to hold the space on one side and to prevent your opponent from interfering with the pass out from the shooter (see Fig 130). Have the ability to reposition on the circle edge by using good footwork and speed to pull off the circle and yet regain another strong position at another point where you are more available to your shooters.

5. Develop line-awareness when taking a high pass into a corner region. Try to take the catch so you are as close to the circle as possible as this will allow you to then make an undefended pass in to your shooters.

6. Be available at an attacking back-line throw-in; hold favourable positions according to where the throw is taken from as seen in Figs 131 and 132. Develop a quick return ball to help your shooter.

7. Develop the ability to receive a centre pass; offer variety by being able to get free in many different ways. Either by fast sprints – have the ability to take the ball, turning inwards towards the centre or outwards away from the centre depending on the closeness of the defenders; by using a reverse pivot in order to change from being inside to being outside your opponent; or by attacking from a position off the third line particularly if you are also marked by the opposing centre. Use a feint dodge in order to attack from either side of your opponent. (See Fig 133.)

8. Develop the ability to contribute defensively when possession is lost. Mark the wing defence from a back-line throw. If you are unable to stop the first pass, defend her pass by marking in front

Fig 133   The WA pulls off the line to release herself from the double marking.

Fig 134   Keep her in the corner and away from the play.

and then face mark her in order to prevent her from moving down the court to be further involved in the attack as shown in Fig 134.

CENTRE

This is an important position – it is the link position which converts defensive possession into attacking power. It is also the position from where the ball is delivered at the team's centre pass and therefore it is vital that the player can give an accurate pass in order to set the attack into action. An ability to read the game and make wise decisions as to when to get involved in the play and when to reposition is also an asset. If the player runs all over the place she makes it difficult for her own players and puts excessive fitness demands on her own performance. The fact that she has the greatest area of the court to work in means that she can have a great influence on the game, but it must be disciplined and controlled. She can play a very important role in controlling the pace of the game by choosing to speed it up or slow it down when the state of the game demands and when it is in her own team's interest to change the pace. Obviously it needs a 'thinking player' to play in this position, as her performance will reflect on the performance of her whole team.

Hints and Tips

1. Develop good communication skills with the centre court players so that you are able to give them the correct type of centre pass according to their positioning and that of their opponent. Be prepared to make the pass to any of the centre court players but, in particular, to the wing attack or goal attack. Use the defending players only as an occasional alternative or when the attacking players are having particular difficulties.

2. Take time to consider your move after the centre pass and react according to the movements of the other players. You should remain as a back-up if required (see Fig 135) or choose the space avail-

able and try to attack the circle. Do not follow the path of the ball. (See Figs 136 and 137.)

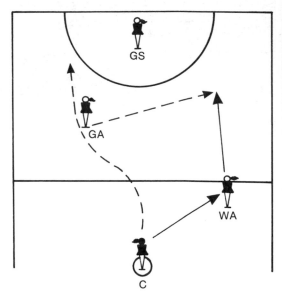

Figs 136 & 137   Choose space wisely – here it is to the left of the circle, and in Fig 137 it is to the right.

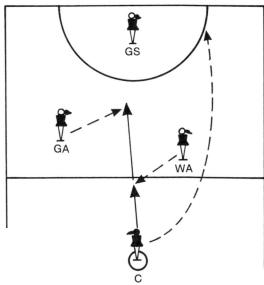

Fig 137.

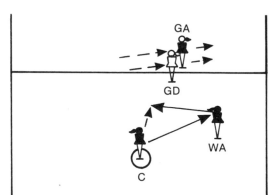

Fig 135   The C is ready to back up the WA when the GA is having difficulty.

Fig 138   Sue Collins (England) keeps a strong hold on the edge of the circle.

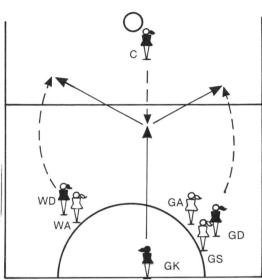

Fig 140   C assesses the situation before coming into the goal third to take the first pass.

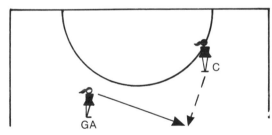

Fig 139   The centre increases her availability by pulling off the circle.

3.   Be available around the circle if needed, cither by hugging the circle edge strongly – keep a wide, firm stance to prevent interference by your opponent, as seen in Fig 138, by constant repositioning around the circle in order to gain superiority or by pulling off the circle to increase availability. (See Fig 139.)

4.   Be available within the centre third by moving to receive a pass from the defending players if the opposing attack breaks down, watch the wing defence and do not take her space.

5.   Try to be available to take a pass from the back-line throw-in if the defending players are being closely marked and are

in difficulties as illustrated in Fig 140. Make your move from the centre third, receiving the ball within the goal third but only do this in an emergency, as the defending players would normally be expected to take this first pass. Remember to reposition after you have thrown the next pass.

6.   Make the following decisions at your opposing team's centre pass in order to make it as difficult as possible for them to give an accurate pass:

(a)   defend the opposing wing attack;
(b)   defend the centre from a distance of 0.9m (3ft), particularly if she is small or has a low release point on her throw;
(c)   take a central position between the goal attack and wing attack and make a late decision.

7.   Be prepared to go back to defend when your team loses possession. Try to

make an interception or mark very tightly, particularly around the circle. Try to cut off the straight pass-in, as this will help your defenders.

8. Be alert for tips or deflections out of the circle by your defenders. Take your time to begin your team's attack and then reposition as you move down the court. You might not be needed, so do not crowd the area by rushing at full speed from one circle area to the other.

WING DEFENCE

This is, in my opinion, the most difficult position on the court. It requires tenacity, concentration and a full range of defending skills, as well as a range of attacking skills in order to help in bringing the ball down the court. It also requires an ability to read the game in order to make it as difficult as possible for the ball to enter the shooting circle. An alert and effective wing defence makes the job of the circle defenders so much easier. I was privileged in my own playing career to play behind a player who knew how to play the position very well and although I received the glory for the interceptions which I was able to make, they were the result of the terrier-like persistency and hard work of the wing defence, who was the cause of the opposition's less than accurate feeds into the circle.

Hints and Tips

1. Exert pressure on the opposing wing attack, at the centre pass, by marking very closely and attempt to make the interception or to drive her towards the side-line and out of the court area – try to reduce the space available to her.

2. If No. 1 proves an unsuccessful move then attempt to defend the wing attack from a position that prevents her from reaching her prime area – the edge of the attacking circle. This means defending her from a position 0.9m (3ft) when she is holding the ball, then face marking her from in front after she has released the ball to prevent her from moving down the court – second, and third stage defending.

3. Link-up with your centre to prevent their wing attack from taking the centre pass. Be prepared to switch opponents and to mark the opposing centre if she successfully manages to get the ball to another player.

4. Always try to be between your opponent and her shooters in order to prevent the straight pass into the shooting circle. Make your stance as wide as possible in order to make it as difficult as possible for the ball to pass through. Watch the positioning of the goal shooter in order to spot where she is requesting the pass and try to cover that possibility. Try to cover her free side but remember to be at least 0.9m (3ft) away from the thrower's landing foot as shown in Fig 141.

5. Move around the circle to prevent your opponent from gaining the strong available position which she is hoping to gain. Be prepared to be constantly changing your position in order to confuse your opponent.

6. Make decisions as to whether it would be better to mark your opponent in front or to drop on to the circle edge. Communicate with your circle defenders as to what they would prefer.

7. Be ready for tips and deflections out of the circle by your defenders as illustrated in Fig 142 and be prepared to set up the next attack.

8. Be available to receive a back-line

Fig 141 WD covers the straight pass in to the GS.

Fig 142 Sue Keal (England) waits for possible tips out by her defenders.

throw-in, again learn to communicate with your other defenders; or be prepared to take the second pass.

Look and learn to use space wisely. Be aware of the movements of your other players and do not take space that is about to be filled by another of your own players. If you are not required, be prepared to back up the attack through the centre court and be prepared to receive a back pass on the two-thirds line if your attackers are struggling and need some help.

GOAL DEFENCE

This is an exciting position which requires speed, anticipation and good elevation. Add to this concentration, tenacity and an

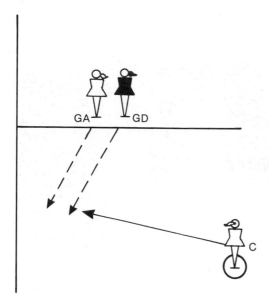

Fig 143   Go strongly for that interception.

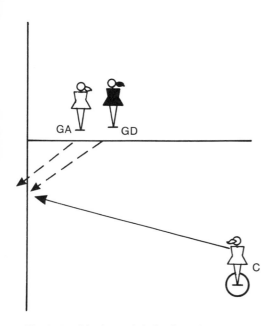

Fig 144   Mark so tightly that she goes out of court.

ability to read the flow of the game and you have a very special player. The position requires the use of all the defending skills as well as an ability to work as a team with the other players in order to make it as difficult as possible for the opponents to penetrate the circle area. After achieving possession the goal defence needs all the attacking skills in order to be instrumental in the safe passage of the ball from the defending zone to her own team's attacking space.

Hints and Tips

1. Develop the skills of defending your opponent at the centre pass either by making the interception shown in Fig 143, or by driving her out of court as in Fig 144. If you are unsuccessful defend her after she has received the ball in order to try to intercept her next pass or to keep her in the centre third after she has released the ball; this is a useful tactic if she is a faster player than you and an important player within their attack.
2. Develop the marking technique which will prevent the goal attack from getting into the shooting circle. Try to cover any pass that she may make from a position 0.9m (3ft) in front of her – second stage defending. Encourage her to make rash decisions and then after she has released the ball, try to prevent her from moving forward by moving into a position between her and the goal-post. Delaying her progress is the third stage of defending.
3. Be alert for possible interceptions and practise moving from a close-marking position to be able to pick up speed in order to attempt the interception of a pass meant for another player as seen in Figs 145 and 146. This requires good footwork and reading of the game. Don't

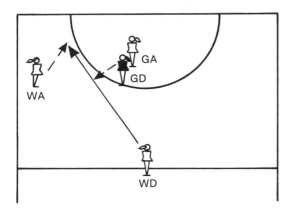

Figs 145 & 146   Be brave and go for the interception.

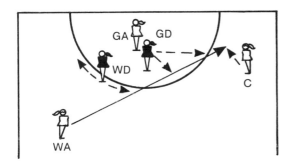

Fig 146   Tempt the pass before making your move.

Fig 147   Link with your GK to double mark out of the game.

be put off if you get it wrong on some occasions; experience will teach you when to try and when not to but it is so exciting when you get it right.

4.   Be proficient at all methods of defending, coming from the side, from in front and from the rear. Defend any shots at goal. Find out which method suits you and is most successful against your opponent. Remember to turn and rebound any missed shots.

5.   Be prepared to work with the goalkeeper, switching opponents when necessary. Be prepared to double-mark one player if she is having too great an influence on the game or she is scoring all the goals. (*See* Fig 147.) At all times talk to

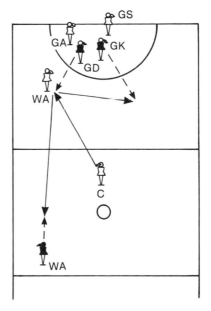

Fig 148   After the exciting interception be calm and select wisely.

each other, as well as to the wing defence in order to make it as difficult as possible for the attacking players.

6. Be available to receive the first pass from a back-line throw-in in order to set your team on to the attack. Be prepared to help or back up the movement of the ball through the centre court. Watch your spacing and do not take other players' space. Remember that you are the back-up player – to be used only if needed.

7. Be prepared to turn an exciting interception into an attacking movement.

Remember that many a bad pass can follow a good interception so take your time and select wisely in order to allow your own players to reposition. (*See* Fig 148.)

GOALKEEPER

This is the hard working, grafting position, requiring all the skills of defending, but the goalkeeper's reactions need to be so much faster as the ball is normally travelling over a short distance and time is limited. Being tall and having the ability to jump high and vertically are useful assets for playing this position but equally important are good footwork and mobility. The goalkeeper is in the best position to see and read the game as the ball is passed down the court. Much of her work is done before the ball reaches the vulnerable area, when the attacking players are looking to pass the ball into the shooting circle. Good early positioning and repositioning can give the goalkeeper a distinct advantage over her opponent. It is up to her to dictate the positioning and not be at the mercy of attacking players. This particularly applies when taking up the position under the post for rebounding a missed shot.

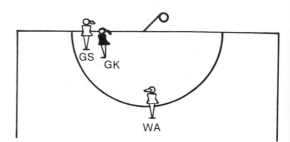

Figs 149–51   Away from the post.

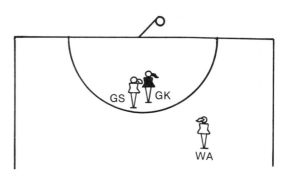

Fig 150   Out of the circle.

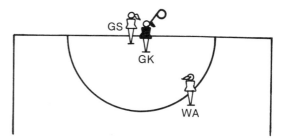

Fig 151   Close to the back-line forcing her out of court.

Hints and Tips

1. Place yourself in the following positions to give your opponent, their goal shooter, as little space as possible to

move about in and only offer her the least desirable space such as Fig 149 (away from the ball and the post), Fig 150 (out of the circle) or Fig 151 (off the back-line).

2. Force tall shooters away from the goal-post. They are normally less accurate with longer shots. They also tend to lack the mobility required to get back under the post.

3. Be prepared to attempt an interception when you see the possibility by leaving your own opponent and attempting to cut off a pass to another member of the opposition. Be brave, but also be prepared to cope with the consequences if you get it wrong. Try to delay the next pass from your successful opponent by covering and delaying her next throw to give your own players time to cover for you – second stage defending.

4. Cover any shot at goal and be prepared to turn to prevent your opponent from following in and give yourself the best chance to rebound a missed shot.

5. Take up a strong, firm stance under the post when the goal attack is shooting and give yourself the best chance to jump vertically to reclaim any rebound.

6. Work with your goal defence and wing defence to provide intercepting

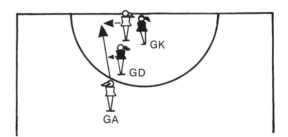

Fig 152   Driving your opponent out to the right can create an interception opportunity for your GD.

possibilities for each other. Drive your opponent behind your own defending players. (*See* Fig 152.)

7. Exert pressure on any attacking back-line throw-in and certainly do not allow the ball to be received close to the post. Work with your goal defence to force the pass out of the circle or at least force a long shot at the goal.

8. Be positive in your selection of the player to throw to when taking a back line throw-in and be prepared to back up to take a return ball if needed.

Whatever position you choose to play remember you are part of a team and success will only come when you and your team-mates help and support each other.

Summary
- There are seven positions in a netball team. Each requires different skills but all are equally important if a team is to be a winning team.
- Young players should be encouraged to play several positions until they make a final decision on where they play best.
- Some players are better at attacking and will favour the attacking positions of centre, wing attack and goal attack. Others will be stronger when defending and will choose to play wing defence, goal defence or goalkeeper. Some are very accurate shooters and will choose to play goal shooter or goal attack.
- In netball, it helps to be tall to play in the circle areas.
- All players must practise to gain the specific skills that are required for each position.

6 Team-Work

Performing the individual skills and knowing how to play a position are necessary attributes of a good netball player, but unless the player is able to blend her skills with those of her team-mates then her own specialized skills will be wasted. During a game each player has her own restricted area of movement and although her area may overlap with that of another player, no one player can have a dominating influence on the result of a game. An accurate shooter is very desirable but she can only contribute if the other players within her team are able to bring the ball down to her inside the circle. A dominant defender is only effective if the rest of her team are able to convert her good interceptions into successful passing moves down the court and into the circle to score a goal. Netball can therefore be described as a genuine team game because of the need for all the players to be involved. All players have a part to play whether their team is in possession and attacking or when not in possession and defending. In a good team all players will be working together as a unit – this is what is meant by team-work.

ATTACKING TEAM-WORK
(Figs 153–6)

A team becomes the attacking team when it gains possession of the ball. This may occur at a centre pass when the game is restarted after a goal has been scored; it may also occur at a throw-in, when the ball has gone out of court and is returned into play by a throw from outside the boundary lines of the court; or at a free or penalty pass, which has been awarded to your team because of an infringement of the rules by the opposition.

These are known as dead-ball situations – times when the game is restarted from a still or standing position. The team in possession can have a little bit of thinking time in order to put into action attacking plans and strategies. These situations can be well-rehearsed in practice and can show flowing team-work in action.

A less predictable method of becoming the attacking team is when an interception is made during actual play. It is difficult to pre-plan for such situations, particularly when the interception is of the more spectacular flying type made against the flow of the play. Often the next pass is thrown away because of the unavailability of players who are still moving in the wrong direction and need time to recover. I was lucky enough to coach a player who was able to intercept like this quite regularly and therefore we did, as a team, pre-plan for just such an incident. However, at a normal interception, a good team will be able to pick up planned patterns if all the players are aware of their own role within the team. It is when players all move for the same ball or all move to the same space that difficulties occur.

In order to avoid such overcrowding most attacking team-work is designed to

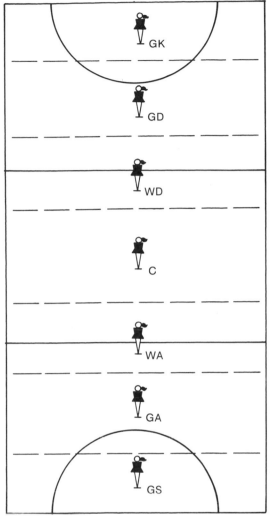

Fig 153   Simple banding across the court.

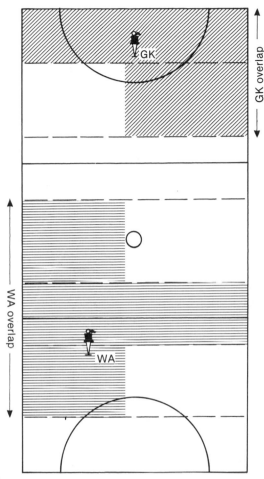

Fig 154   Simple interchanging and overlapping of bands.

create space which will make safe passing easier. This is made possible by using a simple system of court linkage where each player takes responsibility for an area of the court and is given first option on receiving the ball in that area. With beginners it is helpful to try to stick to the use of this simple banding, as it helps each player to be involved and gives her plenty of space in which to make herself free to receive the pass.

Obviously, attacking moves are not always as simple as this and there is a need for interchanging or overlapping of bands. Good communication between the players can make this happen very easily. Ideally every pass should go forward but occasionally the use of a back-up player can help if other players are having difficulties. It allows the original player time to readjust her position and to make another offer to receive the ball. (*See* Fig 155.) Occasionally a player makes a definite run and is deliberately

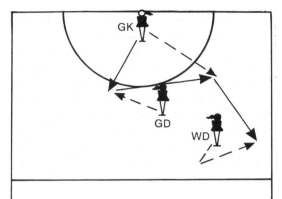

Fig 155   Here a back-up player is used.

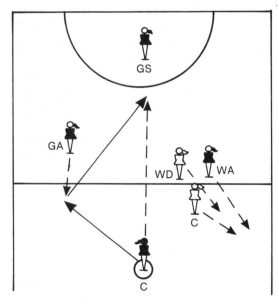

Fig 156   The WA makes a dummy run.

left out. This is called a dummy run and is a useful ploy to occupy defenders and to clear a space for another member of the team to use. (*See* Fig 156.)

In netball most dead-ball situations are based on the simple concept of court linkage.

Throw-ins

Throws from behind the goal-line will normally be the responsibility of the three main defending players. They will be expected to bring the ball down the court into the centre court area. How they do this will depend on the positioning of their opponents, but it could follow any of the following patterns:

(i)   simple court linkage – GK, GD, WD;
(ii) simple interchange – GK, WD, GD;
(iii) use of a back-up player – GK, GD, GK, WD.

The ball could then be passed on to the link player, the centre.

Very occasionally, if both the defenders on court are having difficulty they can make a move to the side. This creates space in the centre of the court for the centre to take the pass from the goal-keeper. The pass must be taken in the goal third. The goal defence or wing defence will then have time to reposition further down the court taking over the role of the link player.

In most cases the centre is the link player between the three defending players and the three attacking players. Her role is to pass the ball on to one of the attacking players, who then pass towards the shooting circle. Again simple court linkage should be in evidence:

(i)   simple court linkage – C, WA, GA, GS;
(ii) simple interchange – C, WA, GS, GA;
(iii) use of a back-up player – C, WA, WD, GA, GS.

If players practise these patterns it is easy during a game to pick one up whenever a throw-in is taken. (*See* Figs 157 & 158.)

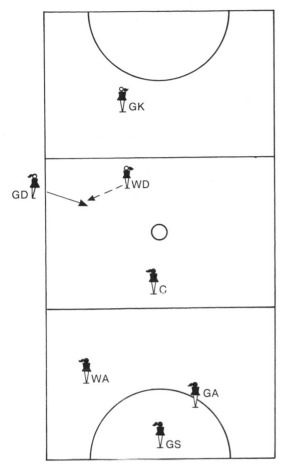

Fig 157   Simple court linkage – GD
passes to WD.

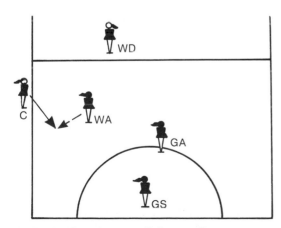

Fig 158   Simple court linkage – C
passes to the WA.

Obviously the pass will be made according to the availability of the players and the positioning of the opponents, who will be doing their utmost to deprive the attacking players of the space which they need. When the throw-in takes place from a position behind the shooting circle then the pattern changes slightly as one of the two shooters will have to take the throw, normally the goal attack. Her main task will be to try to pass to her goal shooter, who is as close as possible to the post. The defenders will be trying to prevent this but the thrower will have other alternatives as her back-up players, the wing attack and centre, will have strong, favourable positions around the goal-circle edge. The goal attack can either make a pass to the goal shooter over the defenders, as in Fig 159; a pass to the unmarked side of the wing attack, who can then return the ball to her after she has returned to the court (see Fig 160); or a pass to the centre who can feed the goal shooter as she turns to face her, as shown in Fig 161.

Free Passes and Penalty Passes

Free passes and penalty passes are awarded for infringements during a game and are awarded to the non-offending team. They can be taken by

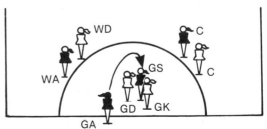

Fig 159   A pass to the GS over the defenders.

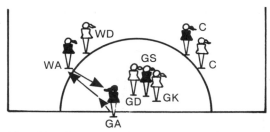

Fig 160   A pass to the unmarked side of the WA.

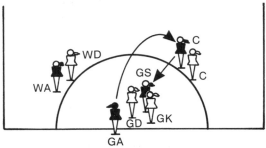

Fig 161   A pass to the C who can then feed the GS with ease.

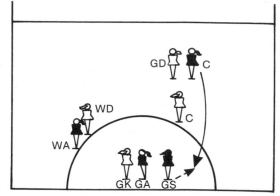

Fig 162   The GA protects the space for the GS.

any member of that team providing they can play in the area where the infringement happened. Penalty passes are specifically awarded for offences involving contact and obstruction. They differ from free passes in that the offending player must stand beside the penalty taker and must not move until the ball has left the thrower's hands. This obviously gives a great advantage to the attacking team as it gives them an extra player until the penalty pass has been taken.

As any player can take these passes a team can very easily pick up on simple court linkage to bring the ball quickly down the court. The penalty pass is made easier by the availability of an undefended player – particularly when the offending player is a circle defender and the offence takes place outside the circle. (See Fig 162.) The player who is taking

the penalty must be quick to spot the opportunity.

Centre Passes

The ideal centre pass aims to transfer the ball forward, with as few passes as possible, from the centre to the goal shooter or goal attack within the circle, to create a shooting opportunity. Normally this will involve the main attacking players, the centre, the wing attack, the goal attack and the goal shooter. Again simple court linkage should be in evidence:

(i)   simple court linkage – C, WA, GA, GS;
(ii) simple interchange – C, GA, WA, GS, or C, WA, GS, GA;
(iii) use of a back-up player – C, WA, C, GA, GS.

At first these passes can be practised without opponents and then with opponents. The players need to learn where they are going, when they are going, where they are starting from and where they are going after they have released the ball. This is the basis of team-work and should lead the team to use their

90

court space well. This gives the players a good grounding to progress from and if their opponents position themselves in such a way, it will allow the team to take advantage and be successful.

However, netball is an unpredictable game and most of the unpredictability is caused by the defending players. They will obviously be trying to prevent the free passage of the ball into the circle. The better the defenders, the more difficult it will be. The attacking team always has the upper hand as they have the ball. Yet they still need to be flexible and adaptable and must be prepared to look at the whole court scene to make decisions as to which moves would be more favourable to their team. Each player is involved in this decision-making and provided that there is good communication between the players the correct decisions will be made. The team will win as a result of team-work!

Decision-making

It is worth looking at each player's vision and thinking when faced by opponents who are trying to make things as difficult as possible.

SITUATION 1 *(Fig 163)*

Centre
'I will easily get the ball to the wing attack.'
'The goal attack looks well positioned to take the next pass.'
'There will be space to the left of the circle after the goal attack has made her move.'
'I will move slowly forward in case I am needed again and then I will aim to be available if required in the space to the left of the circle.'

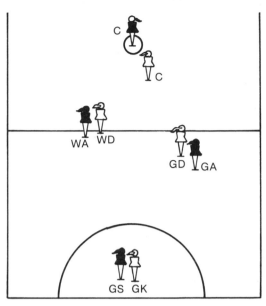

Fig 163   Situation 1.

Wing Attack
I am well positioned to take this centre pass.'
'My goal attack is favourably positioned to take the next pass.'
'If she doesn't make it, my centre is my back-up.'
'I will fill the space to the right or on the crown of the circle depending on where the goal attack takes the ball, so that I am available if I am needed again.'

Goal Attack
'My wing attack is in an ideal position to receive the centre pass.'
'I can afford to begin positioning to be available to move to make the second pass either to the centre or right of the circle.'
'My goal shooter is in a good position for a quick pass in.'

Goal Shooter
'The centre pass looks as if it will go to the wing attack.'

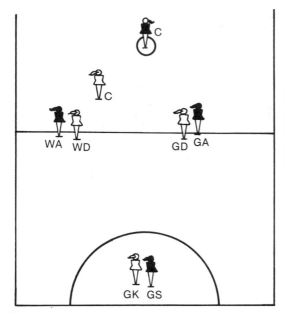

Fig 164   Situation 2.

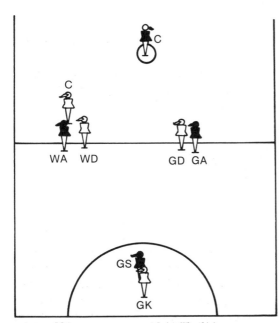

Fig 165   Situation 3.

'It looks as if the ball will come in to the circle on my left side.'
'I will try to keep my opponent on the opposite side.'

SITUATION 2 *(Fig 164)*
This vision and thinking changes when the centre is faced with a wing attack who has been forced more towards the sideline and a goal attack who has achieved a more favourable position. Consider what your decisions would be in this situation.

SITUATION 3 *(Fig 165)*
This vision and thinking changes again when the centre is faced with a wing attack who is being marked not only by her own opponent but also by the centre. Decide on what action you would take this time.

A good team needs skilful players but it also needs thinking players who can react to what they see. They need to make decisions on what is best for their team and make movements accordingly. Communication between the players is vital for good team-work. Compare the decisions you made in the previous decision-making situations with the following answers but remember there are many alternatives.

SITUATION 1 *(Fig 166)*
The centre passes to WA who passes to GA, GA to GS; *see* basic court linkage as given on page 90.

SITUATION 2 *(Fig 167)*
The centre passes to GA who passes to WA, WA to GS. The GA took the initiative as she was better positioned. The WA made a move, changed direction and then freed herself to take the second pass on the crown of the circle where she was able to feed GS, who was offering space

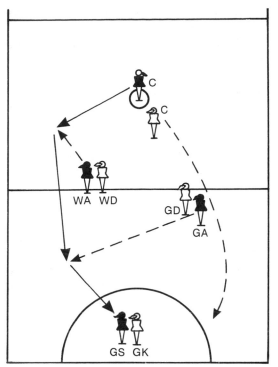

Fig 166   Situation 1.

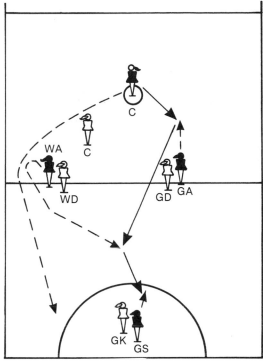

Fig 167   Situation 2.

to her right. Then C moved to fill the space to the right of the circle in case she was needed. (*See* simple interchange as given on page 90.)

SITUATION 3 *(Fig 168)*

The centre passes to GA who returns it to C, C to GS. The goal attack moved to take the centre pass. The wing attack made a determined move into the centre third and took both defending players with her – a dummy run. This left space in the middle for the centre to take a return pass and throw into the goal shooter who was holding space to the front of her.

Whatever the situation in the game, in order to get the best out of it, all players must be aware of their role within the team. They must be prepared to work for each other and to communicate, and to react quickly and decisively. When all of this happens you have good, attacking team-work.

DEFENDING TEAM-WORK *(Fig 169)*

If attacking is about creating space in order to reduce the chances of errors and possible interceptions then defending is about the closing down of space by getting as many players in an area as possible in order to force errors and to make interceptions more likely. If possession is lost all members of the team become defenders – the main aim is to regain

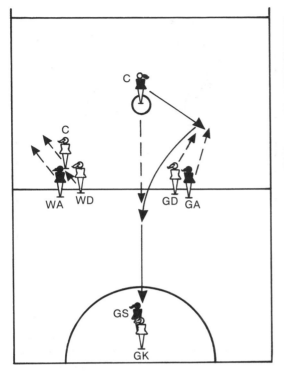

Fig 168   Situation 3.

Fig 169   Circle defenders reduce space for the attacking players.

possession. All of the team must be proficient in the three stages of defending and must be prepared to work on their own in a man-to-man defence, or to link up with one or more players to form a small-zone defence or to work as a team using a full-zone defence when and if required.

All players need to understand that success will be achieved if they are spatially aware, particularly of what is less desirable space such as movement towards the boundary lines, movement into corners, movement away from the thrower, movement away from the post or movement behind one of your own players. As each pass is made the less desirable space changes and therefore each defender must be constantly changing her position in order to confuse the thrower. They also need to realize that a lot of players in one area causes difficulties for the attacking players and therefore it is desirable to get as many defending players behind the ball as possible.

Man-to-Man Defending

This is a basic method of defending when each player takes the responsibility of defending her own opponent. In this way pressure is exerted on both the thrower and the catcher as the ball travels down the court. It is very difficult to give equal concentration to all three stages of defending at the same time. As a team, therefore, you may choose to exert pressure on the first and third stage or second and third stage defending. Alternatively you may have some players being particularly heavy on one stage. Goal defence may concentrate on third stage against

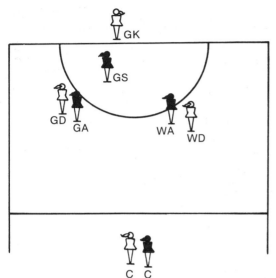

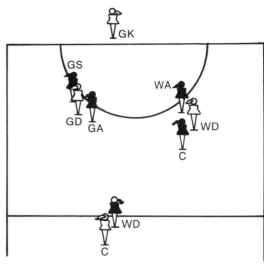

Fig 171.

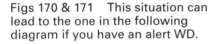

Figs 170 & 171   This situation can lead to the one in the following diagram if you have an alert WD.

her opponent in order to keep her out of the circle, whereas others may be dropping off to invite the pass and hope to make a late move to take the interception.

Man-to-man defending can be adapted by the double marking of one player if it is felt that she is having too great an influence on the game. It may be useful for the wing defence to try to prevent the goal attack from entering the circle, leaving the goal defence to help the goalkeeper in preventing the goal shooter from receiving the ball close to the post. Other players can help by slowing the entry of the GA into the circle. The centre would work with the wing defence in order to prevent the opposing wing attack from receiving the centre pass. WD and C may switch opponents if the C manages to get the ball away to another player and may pick her up as she moves up the court.

A further adaptation is the shock tactic of double marking more than one player at a time. This is best done at a dead-ball situation when players have time to read the game and respond to what they see. For example when defending a back-line throw-in the situation in Fig 170 can lead to the situation shown in Fig 171.

Figs 170 and 171 are good examples of effective communication and team-work, but it can only happen when the opposing centre takes up a position well into the centre third. The defending wing defence can set it in motion by taking up a defending position in front of the centre and therefore preventing her from moving towards and into the goal third. Remember that the rules say that the first pass must be caught or touched within the goal third. This gives the defending centre the opportunity to link up with the wing attack in exerting pressure on the wing defence. The goal attack and goal shooter will have already joined forces to pressurize the goal defence. The result is usually a panic throw from the goalkeeper, when she is unable to see a clear, free player. An interception so close to the shooting circle can prove very valuable.

Zone Defending

Whereas man-to-man defending requires a total focus of attention on one player, with a late shift to the ball once it is in the air, zone defending requires the total focus of attention to be on the ball and its passage through the space. It is normally used to upset the play and rhythm of the opposition. It can be very successful over a short period provided that the communication between the players is good enough to switch it on or off. Also it requires a high level of skill and a good awareness of space on the court and the closing down of that space. It therefore tends to be a tactic used only by the more experienced clubs, counties and national squads, though even these tend to rely on the switching on of partial zones rather than full-court zones. New Zealand's national team has proved that it can upset the play of other countries by the use of zone defending. The fact that other national squads do not meet or are not able to practise against this method, has led to New Zealand achieving the status of World Champions. Other nations seem to rely on a mixture of partial zones and good man-to-man defending.

PARTIAL ZONES

Taking a four player defensive zone in the goal third as an example we see partial zones at work. As shown in Fig 172 the GK and GD split the circle, WD and C cover the front of the circle moving according to the position of the ball. In this way the straight ball into the circle is always cut off by a player on the edge of the circle. This may be varied by the other defender putting pressure on the free player who hopes to receive the pass. (*See* Fig 173.)

This requires many build-up practices aimed at preventing the ball passing through a space. It also requires the players to be agile, mobile and very fit in order to cover the necessary ground. Concentration levels also need to be high

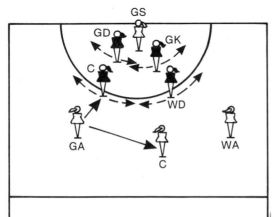

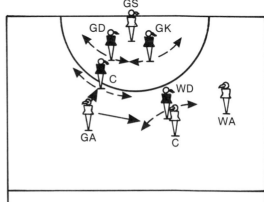

Figs 172 & 173   A four player defensive zone.

Fig 173   A slight variation on Fig 172 exerting more pressure on the free centre court player.

in order to follow the ball and to read the possible flight paths.

A centre court partial zone involves the placing of a barrier across the court. This is quite difficult to do because of the size of the area but if achieved it can be quite effective, particularly as a shock tactic. (*See* Fig 174.) The GS and GA attempt to mark as normal from the back-line throw but if they are unsuccessful in preventing the ball reaching the GD or WD, they immediately drop back on to the third line. The WD, C and WA form a line behind them and the GD

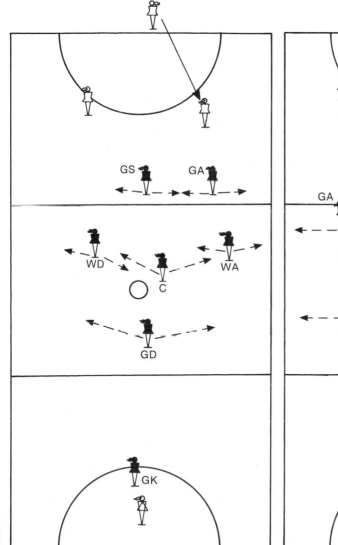

Fig 174   A centre court partial zone.

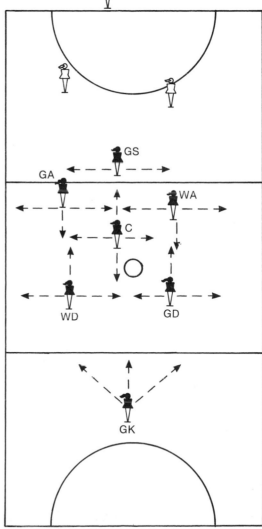

Fig 175   The full-court zone.

moves freely along the back in case the attacking team throw a long ball over the top. From then on they concentrate on the flight of the ball rather than on the opponents.

It requires a great deal of discipline from all players to move into their positions when the signal is given. One forgetful player and the zone does not work.

FULL-COURT ZONE

There are many methods of setting up a full-court zone but the one in Fig 175 proves very successful. It involves getting as many players in one area as possible. This makes the passage of the ball through that area very difficult. As soon as the ball comes close to the third line, the player in possession is put under pressure by having a player in front of her. At all times, as an attempt is made to bring the ball down the court, the player in possession is not allowed to pass forward. This results in many sideways passes or the hasty attempt to throw over the top – both of which provide interception chances for the defending team. In all cases each player must know her role and must be able to change tactics when the appropriate cues are given.

Slipping in and out of a zone is always the most difficult part and this is when team-work is so important. The switch from player-watching to ball-watching is

Fig 176   The New Zealand zone in action.

also difficult, making the use of this skill an advanced tactic.

Whatever your team decides to do the main principle must always be to do what will most upset the play of your opponents in order to gain success for your own team. This may mean constantly changing ploys but it may equally mean sticking to the same one if it proves effective.

Summary
- Good attacking depends on good use of space.
- Teams should practise working together to bring the ball down the court from set positions in the game: from a centre pass, throw-in or free pass/penalty pass situation.
- Good defending depends on all players working as a team to close down the space and make it difficult for the attacking team to progress up the court.

Defenders must work with a plan to make the opposition think. They can:
- close man-to-man mark.
- 2 on 1 mark in some areas of the court.
- set up a partial zone.
- set up a full-court zone.
- Teams need to train together regularly to be able to communicate and make the right decisions at the right time during the game.

7 Fitness Training

Anyone can learn the skills of netball by following the skill practices in this and other books. However, to be able to perform efficiently throughout the whole game, a player must have a high fitness level. She must be able to run, jump, throw, change direction and generally keep up an excellent level of performance under the continual pressure of opponents who are equally as talented. This requires cardiovascular and muscular endurance, speed, strength, suppleness and mobility; all highly trainable components of fitness.

In order to plan a fitness programme for players, the coach must have basic knowledge of how movement is produced. It is produced by energy which is stored in the muscles; as the muscle contracts it draws on this supply and it is therefore necessary for this to be easily replenished.

ENERGY

The body uses up energy in two different ways:

(i) aerobic energy – this is the energy used for continuous movement and therefore it is an important source for any activity which requires stamina and staying power. A basic requirement of this energy system is oxygen and this is delivered to the muscle via the lungs, the heart and the blood vessels. There it reacts with the glucose from food to create usable energy.

Provided enough oxygen is supplied, through efficient breathing, an abundant source of energy should be available;

(ii) anaerobic energy – this is the energy used for sudden and intensive movement and it is therefore important for activities which require short sharp bursts of movement. This energy supply does not require immediate access to oxygen but makes use of fuel already stored in the muscle. This store is small and is quickly used up when an instant energy supply is needed. A by-product of this energy source is the production of lactic acid which unfortunately quickly interferes with the muscular contractions and causes the muscle to feel tired. The player quickly recovers after a short rest when extra supplies of oxygen have been taken into the lungs and help to rebuild the store of energy. At the same time the lactic acid is removed via the blood and vascular system.

It is important to realize that an efficient aerobic system helps to clear and replenish the anaerobic system during rest periods.

The game of netball includes movements which are short, sharp and high in intensity followed by periods of short rest. Research by L. Otago in 1983, has shown that these movements tend to be of no more than ten seconds in length, the majority of them being of less than four seconds. These movements are normally followed by short rest periods which allow for the replenishing of energy stores.

In 1977 a survey was done on the England team; it made an attempt to analyse the aerobic and anaerobic energy uses of different playing positions during a one hour match. The results were only estimates but they provided evidence that in all players, except the goal attack and goal defence, the balance was much more towards anaerobic energy use rather than aerobic. The implication for a training programme is that short bursts of high intensity training followed by short rests must form a major part of the programme. It is also a fact that with good training the body can learn to tolerate an oxygen debt for longer periods.

It should be remembered, however, that the anaerobic energy is replenished more quickly if the oxygen supply to the body is efficient. As mentioned on page 100 a good aerobic system will lead to a quicker recovery. This involves training with constant activity in order to develop the cardiovascular and respiratory system. Continuous running and skipping activities which will raise the pulse rate and keep it raised must also be a necessary part of the training scheme.

Alongside our training to increase the efficiency of our energy supplying systems, we must also train to improve our strength, speed and suppleness.

Fig 177   Netball players need strength.

improved by the use of carefully prepared circuit training, with or without the use of weights, and by the use of bounding and hopping type activities.

STRENGTH

Netball demands hard work on legs, arms and the body. An increase in the strength of muscle will enable the player to jump higher, throw further and more powerfully and to move more explosively. Bursts of power and speed are all valuable parts of the game. Strength can be

SPEED

Speed on the court, so you can outrun an opponent or intercept a pass by the opposition, is a vital component of fitness. This short burst speed, together with a quick reaction speed, are also easily trainable and can be catered for within a training programme by the use of circuit training, short burst sprint and recovery practices and by quick reaction drills.

101

Fig 178　Netball players need speed.

SUPPLENESS

During a game of netball the player is asked to twist and turn her body. She has to cope with uneven landings, off-balance situations and reaching out and stretching joints to their limits. Without suppleness and mobility training the body will be likely to break down when put under this constant strain. Slow stretching exercises and mobility work will help to increase the blood flow and therefore the oxygen supply to the muscles. This will warm the muscles, make them more elastic and generally prepare them for more violent activity. For this reason stretching and mobility exercises normally take place at the beginning of each training session and form a major part of any warm-up routine. A stretched and warmed-up muscle is less likely to break down when doing more explosive work.

If all of these fitness components can be achieved with a well-prepared training programme, then the skills of the game will be performed more efficiently. This is illustrated by the following quotations: 'Whatever the ability of the player, she can only do justice to her full potential if she is in peak condition.' P. Edwards and S. Campbell *Netball Today* (Lepus Books, 1981).

'Fatigue is a factor which impairs both the learning and the performance of netball skills.' H. Crouch *Netball Coaching Manual* (A &C Black, 1984).

TYPES OF TRAINING

Steady Runs

These can vary between one and five miles. A shorter run should be attempted at the best possible speed – a quality run; whereas the longer distance can be run at a slightly slower pace.

Fartlek Runs

These are runs with a varied pace. Short, faster bursts of twenty to one hundred and twenty seconds are included within a steady run. Other activities which can be introduced are changes in direction, driving off the right foot, driving off the left foot, jumps, twists or turns. Any activity which is relevant to the game can be added at various intervals.

Interval Work

This is the completion of a set distance in

a given time with a fixed rest or recovery period before the next exercise. Monitoring the heart rate after warming up is an important part of this training. It can be done in three ways:

(i) complete the activity, then rest until the heart rate returns to normal and then complete the activity again. Repeat the procedure eight times;
(ii) repeat (i) but begin again before the heart rate has reached its former level;
(iii) continuous activity keeping the rest interval so short that the heart rate falls only slightly between activities.

Examples to achieve this are sprint 20m (20yds), rest until heart rate returns to normal, repeat eight times; sprint 20m (20yds), walk or jog back to the start, repeat eight times and sprint 20m (20yds), slow down, turn and sprint back. Repeat eight times.

Shuttle Runs

These can vary tremendously and need not be 'there and back' types but can involve other activities such as twists, turns, jumps, throws and shots. Various examples are given on pages 110–11.

Circuits

These are circuits of activities where the player moves from one activity to another. The time spent at each activity may be of a set period of time or the activity may have to be repeated a certain number of times. This may be a general number for everyone on the circuit or it may be an individual number that has been worked out earlier by the coach. The circuit may be aimed at certain elements of fitness, such as stamina, strength or speed, depending on the specific needs of the individual or the group. The circuit itself may take the form of traditional exercise using little or no equipment, a skills circuit or a combination of skills and exercise. It could also be a circuit using loose weights or the stations of a multi-gym. If you choose to use weights you should always seek guidance from professionals at a reputable centre. Examples of other circuits are given later on in this chapter on pages 112–16.

Whatever you choose to do in your training session, each one must be preceded by a full warm-up in a track suit. Items should be removed as the warm-up progresses through jogging, striding and stretching. Gradually build up until your muscles are able to work at the speed which you will require of them in training or in a match. The blood and the muscles should be warm with the muscles more elastic and much more ready to react to intensive activity.

After activity the cool-down is equally important. This should be done at the end of each session in a track suit. Keep your body moving until your normal body temperature is achieved. Finish off by stretching, to check that the muscles have retained their flexibility and the joints their mobility. Only when you feel comfortable and relaxed should you have your shower.

MONITORING FITNESS

When exercise begins the heart beats faster. The speed at which it increases is dependent on several things:

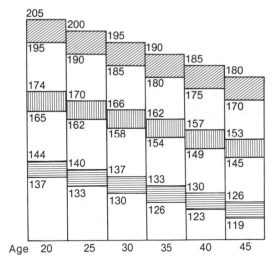

100% maximum heart rate possible (exhaustion)

85% generally recommended level

70% minimum level for training effect

Fig 179 Guide to heart rates.

time. A 70 per cent raising of the pulse rate is the minimum level for any training effect on the body and most coaches would be aiming for an 85 per cent increase.

With suitable training the heart returns to resting rate faster and the resting heart rate should drop because the heart has become more efficient and is able to perform the same work with less effort. It may be worthwhile for a player to build into the fitness programme pulse counting, as it is a way of proving to the coach that the programme is working and to the player that she is benefiting from the hard work.

PLANNING A FITNESS PROGRAMME

Any fitness programme should include the following elements:

(i)   work to increase stamina;
(ii) work with short bursts of activity followed by a decreasing recovery time;
(iii) working when tired, coping with an oxygen debt and building up lactic tolerance;
(iv) work to strengthen muscles;
(v). work to increase suppleness and mobility.

The coach needs to be especially aware of three particular points:

(i)   the need to plan the fitness work so that the player works at a higher intensity than she would meet in a game;
(ii) the need to progress the work as the player gets fitter;
(iii) the need for regular fitness sessions as fitness is difficult to achieve but very

(i)   the type of exercise – the larger the muscle group used, the greater the effect; the more dynamic the exercise, the greater the effect;
(ii) the speed of the exercise;
(iii) the emotional content of the exercise – the amount of pressure and stress;
(iv) the air temperature and humidity;
(v) the physical condition of the player.

The speed at which the heart returns to normal after exercise – the recovery time – is also an indication of the state of the cardiorespiratory fitness of the player. A fitter player will return to normal faster than another player who is unfit. It is generally accepted that the body gains very little from exercise unless the heart rate (pulse) is raised above 120 beats per minute and is kept there for a period of easy to lose. Any large break in training will result in a sharp decline in fitness and it is much easier to maintain a level of fitness than to have to start all over again.

Most club players will give one night a week to training for the weekend match. A county player will give at least two nights. A regional squad player will give more and an international player will be expected to do some sort of training every day except for one rest day. The motivation of these players will vary tremendously and therefore the coach's expectations will also be different. The coach will need to be aware that a whole evening devoted to fitness will not go down very well with the average club player. Time scales become important; as endurance running takes time, after discussing the need for it, players may have to be trusted to do it at another time during the week. During training sessions the coach will need to include variety and fun in order to keep the players interested and motivated. Competition against themselves, against each other or against the clock, will help in achieving this but the keeping of records and the feed-back to the players of their progress will also help to keep up their interest.

As the season progresses, skill work and tactics may appear to take a high priority, however, the emphasis should be to ensure that fitness is maintained. Most fitness work can be done holding a ball and this may be much more acceptable to the average club player. Remember that fitness in itself can be very tedious and boring and it is always up to the coach to add interesting elements in order to motivate her players. A good coach improves the fitness levels of players without mentioning the word fitness.

A wise choice of skill routines can maintain the fitness element at the same time as training skills. Remember – if there is no fun in it, there is no future in it.

The time of year will also influence the type of training necessary.

Out of Season

Most good players like to maintain a good level of fitness during the off-season, which appears to be getting shorter in duration. Ideal ways of doing this are either by continuous involvement in a different sport, a programme of jogging which is much more pleasant in summer weather or a programme to build up strength, perhaps a weight-training routine. (*See* Fig 180.)

Pre-season

This programme should be designed to bring the players back to peak condition. Endurance running should be continued but more anaerobic work should be introduced such as shuttle runs and activity circuits.

In-season

Fitness work must be continued otherwise the body will lose its condition. The aerobic work should be maintained by performing short fifteen to thirty minute runs and the anaerobic content should be maintained by work/recovery/work type practices which can be very much more game-related. Strength and power can be continued in the form of circuits which should be lighter than the out-of-season training. It is important, as previously mentioned, that body fitness is maintained as

General fitness	Stamina	Strength	Suppleness
Out of Season	Two to three mile runs Fartlek training	Weight training Circuit training + the playing of alternative sport	Exercise to music Passive stretching
Pre-season	Thirty min runs Work/recovery Shuttle runs Activity routines	Weight training Circuit training Bounding training Hopping activities Jumping activities	Flexibility exercises Passive stretching
In Season	Skill and endurance work Activity based stamina routines Stress and pressure practices Thirty min runs	Individual circuit training Within practice conditioning Bounding and rebounding practices	Stretching Suppleness exercises using a ball Twisting and turning exercises using a ball Extension and agility exercises Warm-ups and warm-downs

Fig 180   General fitness.

the training of skills, tactics and team-work become dominant. Remember that skills will be performed more efficiently if the fitness level is high.

EXAMPLES OF THE DIFFERENT TYPES OF TRAINING

Stretching and Suppleness Training

Always begin with an easy stretch and hold it for ten to thirty seconds. Reach a point of mild tension and try to relax as you hold the stretch. stretch, moving slowly until a mild tension is fel ten to thirty seconds. The get less as you hold; if ease off slightly. Contro so that you are able to as you hold your stretc ing your breath.

BASIC STRETCHES

1. Neck and shoulders
(a) Gently   take   your

easy to lose. Any large break in training will result in a sharp decline in fitness and it is much easier to maintain a level of fitness than to have to start all over again.

Most club players will give one night a week to training for the weekend match. A county player will give at least two nights. A regional squad player will give more and an international player will be expected to do some sort of training every day except for one rest day. The motivation of these players will vary tremendously and therefore the coach's expectations will also be different. The coach will need to be aware that a whole evening devoted to fitness will not go down very well with the average club player. Time scales become important; as endurance running takes time, after discussing the need for it, players may have to be trusted to do it at another time during the week. During training sessions the coach will need to include variety and fun in order to keep the players interested and motivated. Competition against themselves, against each other or against the clock, will help in achieving this but the keeping of records and the feed-back to the players of their progress will also help to keep up their interest.

As the season progresses, skill work and tactics may appear to take a high priority, however, the emphasis should be to ensure that fitness is maintained. Most fitness work can be done holding a ball and this may be much more acceptable to the average club player. Remember that fitness in itself can be very tedious and boring and it is always up to the coach to add interesting elements in order to motivate her players. A good coach improves the fitness levels of players without mentioning the word fitness.

A wise choice of skill routines can maintain the fitness element at the same time as training skills. Remember – if there is no fun in it, there is no future in it.

The time of year will also influence the type of training necessary.

Out of Season

Most good players like to maintain a good level of fitness during the off-season, which appears to be getting shorter in duration. Ideal ways of doing this are either by continuous involvement in a different sport, a programme of jogging which is much more pleasant in summer weather or a programme to build up strength, perhaps a weight-training routine. (*See* Fig 180.)

Pre-season

This programme should be designed to bring the players back to peak condition. Endurance running should be continued but more anaerobic work should be introduced such as shuttle runs and activity circuits.

In-season

Fitness work must be continued otherwise the body will lose its condition. The aerobic work should be maintained by performing short fifteen to thirty minute runs and the anaerobic content should be maintained by work/recovery/work type practices which can be very much more game-related. Strength and power can be continued in the form of circuits which should be lighter than the out-of-season training. It is important, as previously mentioned, that body fitness is maintained as

General fitness	Stamina	Strength	Suppleness	Speed
Out of Season	Two to three mile runs Fartlek training	Weight training Circuit training + the playing of alternative sport	Exercise to music Passive stretching	Interval runs
Pre-season	Thirty min runs Work/recovery Shuttle runs Activity routines	Weight training Circuit training Bounding training Hopping activities Jumping activities	Flexibility exercises Passive stretching	Short sprints Run/rest/run Reaction drills Circuit training
In Season	Skill and endurance work Activity based stamina routines Stress and pressure practices Thirty min runs	Individual circuit training Within practice conditioning Bounding and rebounding practices	Stretching Suppleness exercises using a ball Twisting and turning exercises using a ball Extension and agility exercises Warm-ups and warm-downs	Short sprints Speed work using a ball Pressure speed practices Footwork speed drills Reflex action activities

Fig 180   General fitness.

the training of skills, tactics and team-work become dominant. Remember that skills will be performed more efficiently if the fitness level is high.

EXAMPLES OF THE DIFFERENT TYPES OF TRAINING

Stretching and Suppleness Training

Always begin with an easy stretch and hold it for ten to thirty seconds. Reach a point of mild tension and try to relax as you hold the stretch. Repeat the easy stretch, moving slowly, a little further until a mild tension is felt again. Hold for ten to thirty seconds. The tension should get less as you hold; if it does not then ease off slightly. Control your breathing so that you are able to breathe normally as you hold your stretch but avoid holding your breath.

BASIC STRETCHES

1. Neck and shoulders (Fig 181)
(a) Gently take your cervical spine

through a full range of movement, by putting your chin to your chest and holding, looking up to the ceiling and holding turning your head to the left and holding and then to the right and holding;
(b) shrug your shoulders up towards your ears, hold and lower;
(c) hold your elbows above your head and pull down and hold.

2. Trunk and back (Figs 182 & 183)
(a) Lie on the floor, stretch out your arms and legs and hold the stretch;
(b) slowly and smoothly bend your knees to your chest and your head towards your knees; hold and repeat.

3. Hips and hamstrings (Fig 184)
This may be done standing up or lying on your back; bend one knee to your chest, lightly holding under your knee. You should feel the tension at the back of your thigh; hold and repeat with your other knee.

Fig 181   Neck and shoulder stretch.

Figs 182 & 183   Trunk and back stretch.   Fig 183.

Fig 184   Hip and hamstring stretch.

Fig 185   Lower spine and hamstring stretch.

Fig 186   Quadriceps stretch.

4. Lower spine and hamstrings (Fig 185)
(a) Sit down with your right leg straight and your left leg bent in a hurdling position. Keep your head up and your back flat.
(b) Reach down with both of your hands towards your toes; hold and repeat using opposite leg.

5. Quadriceps (Fig 186)
(a) Standing, bend your knee and hold your foot with your hand ensuring that your heel is kept away from your thigh in order to prevent strain on the knee joint.
(b) Stretch backwards and slightly upwards to feel the tension on the front of your thigh and hip; hold and repeat opposite leg.

6. Calf stretches (Figs 187 & 188)
The calf consists of two muscle groups which pass over the back of the knee and ankle joints. It is important to stretch both muscle groups:

(a) upper calf – lean against a wall or firm object and support your weight on your arms. Keep your toes pointing forward, heels on the floor and your hip straight. Gently push your hips towards the wall; hold and repeat;

(b) lower calf – repeat the position for the upper calf, but this time with the legs slightly bent and hips lowered. Keep your heels firmly on the ground and your toes pointing forwards throughout the exercise; hold and repeat.

STRETCHING USING A BALL

1. Standing with your feet astride, your hands on the ball and the ball on the floor:

(a) roll the ball as far forward as possible and then as far backwards going between your legs; hold at both ends of the stretch;

(b) roll the ball as far to the side as possible and return to the centre and repeat in the opposite direction firstly with your hand nearest to the side with the ball, then with your opposite hand to the side with the ball and finally with both hands staying in contact with the ball throughout the stretch.

Fig 187 Upper calf stretch.

2. Standing up, roll the ball around your body, beginning at your ankles and working up to your head, then change direction.
3. Pass the ball behind your back, flick it into the air and twist to retrieve with the same hand.
4. Stand sideways to a wall and pass the ball behind your back; throw against the wall and retrieve the rebound.
5. Face a wall and pass the ball behind your back and throw against the wall; twist around to retrieve the rebound.
6. Stand with your back to the wall; twist to touch the wall with the ball held in both your hands and then twist to the opposite side.
7. Stand with your back to the wall; twist to throw the ball against the wall six times on each side of your body.

Fig 188 Lower calf stretch.

Fig 189   Full body stretch.

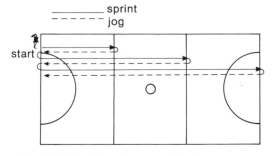

Figs 190–2   Shuttle runs – No. 2.

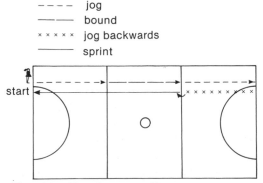

Fig 191   Shuttle runs – No. 5.

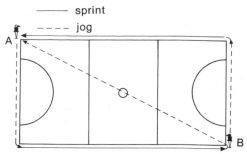

Fig 192   Shuttle runs – No. 6.

8. Sit on the floor with your back to the wall; twist to throw the ball against the wall six times on each side of your body.
9. Sit on the floor and roll the ball around your body, keeping in contact with the floor and at least one hand throughout. Make the biggest circle possible. (*See* Fig 189.)
10. Turn the ball under your arm, pushing upwards and twisting to keep the ball on your hand throughout to return to the starting position.

SHUTTLES *(Figs 190–2)*
1. Sprint five widths of the court; rest for thirty seconds. Repeat five times and gradually reduce your rest period.
2. Sprint to the third line and jog back. Repeat to the furthest third line and finally the full court. Rest for one minute then repeat two more times, gradually aiming to reduce your rest period. (*See* Fig 190.)
3. Do five airborne passes against a wall then bounce the ball across the court and repeat when you reach the opposite side. Do this six times and then rest for thirty seconds and repeat three more times.
4. Do five chest passes against a wall with the sixth throw as an underarm up the wall to be caught whilst you are turning. Bounce the ball across the court and repeat at the other side. Do this five times

and then rest for thirty seconds and repeat three more times.

5. Jog one third of the court, bound the centre third and jog to the end. Change direction to jog backwards for one third, followed by a quick turn and a sprint over the remaining two thirds. Repeat this three times and then rest for thirty seconds; carry on the shuttle for three more times. (*See* Fig 191.)

6. If you have a friend who wants to get fit as well try this one, but it is very hard. Begin at diagonally opposite ends of the court. (*See* Fig 192.) One person (A) jogs the short side and sprints the long side to touch B. Then B jogs the short side and sprints the long side to touch A who has jogged the diagonal to beat B back. B then jogs the diagonal to beat A back and so on.

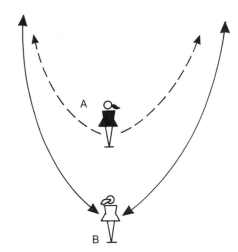

Figs 193–7   Routine No. 1.

SKILL ROUTINES WITH A HEAVY FITNESS INPUT (*Figs 193–7*)

1. A is the worker who bends away to retrieve a lob pass from B, the feeder, and then returns the ball. A then runs back to touch the ball before bending away in the opposite direction. Repeat this twelve times before resting for one minute. Repeat the routine once more (*See* Fig 193).

2. As for Exercise 1 but use a star formation with A moving from 1 – 2 – 3 – 4. A repeats this always returning to the central position; B feeds the ball to each point. The routine should be repeated three times before resting. (*See* Fig 194.)

3. B passes to A; she throws the ball against the wall, catches and returns to B. This is then repeated in the opposite direction. Continue for six more times before resting. (*See* Fig 195.)

4. A jumps five times to touch the net and then sprints to the edge of the circle,

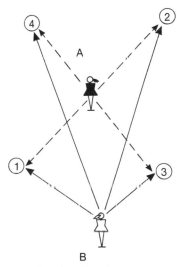

Fig 194   Routine No. 2.

changes direction and takes a pass from B as she moves back towards the post. She returns the ball to B and repeats the routine three times by sprinting to different points on the circle each time.

5. A side-steps along the back line, sprints across the circle, changes

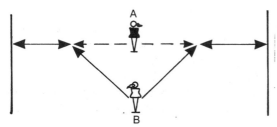

Fig 195   Routine No. 3.

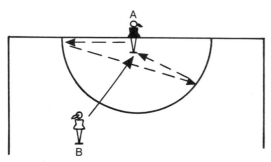

Fig 196   Routine No. 5.

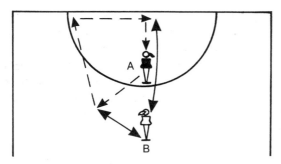

Fig 197   Routine No. 6.

to B, jogs to the circle edge and repeats the routine by sprinting out to the opposite side. (*See* Fig 197.)

CIRCUITS

1.   Basic Exercise Circuit
A circuit can consist of a variety of the following exercises. It is important when planning this circuit that attention is paid to the part of the body which is being used and that you make sure two exercises which use the same muscle groups do not follow each other.

Sit-ups, press-ups, squat jumps, squat thrusts, back arches, burpees, step-ups, straddle-jumps on and off a bench, short shuttle runs, star jumps, etc.

There are two methods of organizing circuits:

(a) all the players do six repetitions of each activity and repeat the circuit twice – building up to completing three circuits; (b) each player works to their own individual scores and records the time taken to complete the circuit, once, twice or even three times. Using this method the coach must work out the individual scores for each player and although it takes time it is a better method, ensuring each individual is stretched.

During the circuit the coach should ensure that each activity is being performed correctly. To work out your scores: work for thirty seconds at each activity, counting the number of repetitions during this time. Halve this personal score and use this number in your circuit. After a period of time, re-test and adjust your scores – you should be improving!

direction and sprints back to take a pass from B near to the post. She then shoots, returns the ball to B and repeats the routine. (*See* Fig 196.)
6.   A sprints out at an angle to catch a pass from B and returns the ball. She then back pedals down to the goal-line before sprinting across to intercept a pass to the post. She then returns the ball

2. Skill and Exercise Circuit (Fig 198)
(a) Use a badminton court, jog to the first service line, sprint to the end of the court, jog backwards to the service line, quick turn and sprint to the end of the court. Repeat five times;
(b) twenty step-ups on to a bench;
(c) twenty chest passes against a wall;
(d) twenty sit-ups;
(e) use a badminton court, side-step the back and service lines, jog the side lines and then sprint back to the start five times;
(f) twenty astride jumps on and off a bench;
(g) twenty shoulder passes against a wall;
(h) twenty two-handed airborne passes against a wall.
Aim to build up from one circuit of (a) – (h) to five.

3. Strength and Stamina Circuit (Fig 199)
Work through this circuit with a partner, one of you working while the other rests and feeds the ball. This is quite a hard circuit and it will be necessary to build up to the required number of repetitions or times;

(a) Begin by the goal post, side-step out to the circle edge and sprint back three times. Jump to touch the net three times. Repeat the whole sequence four times;
(b) the worker guards a marked area, the thrower attempts to throw past the player. Do this for one or two minutes concentrating hard;
(c) stepping on and jumping off a bench ten times with each leg (a feeder can be added to pass the ball caught on the jump);
(d) Sprint from one of the posts to a side-line, jog up a side-line, return towards the post by jumping two-footed over a bench

three times and then sprinting in to catch a ball thrown towards the post. Return the ball to the feeder and repeat the sequence three times;
(e) sprint to A, B and C returning to the start each time by jogging. Repeat this twice. Rest for thirty seconds. Repeat the sprinting twice more before the next rest;
(f) do high ball feeding from two to three metres for two minutes.

4. Stamina Circuit Based on Footwork (Fig 200)
Work through this circuit with a partner who initially acts as a feeder. The whole idea is to be able to work non-stop at each activity for forty-five seconds before changing positions. It is essential to keep your face open to the feeder, who in some cases will decide whether to throw the ball or not. At all times be ready to take a pass if the ball is released:

(a) move out from a position under the goal-post to markers spread around the circle edge, change direction to run back. always watch the feeder who may feed a ball towards the post. Use different foot patterns to cope with the need to always have an open face to the feeder;
(b) sprint out at an angle from the third line as if moving for a centre pass. Receive a pass from the feeder and return it to her. With your back to the side-line quickly side-step down the line, change speed and direction to sprint across and take a pass on the edge of the circle. Return the ball to the feeder, jog back to the third line and repeat;
(c) from one marker, move around each cone in turn always watching the feeder who may pass to you at any of the marked points. Adapt your footwork to cope with the different angle of the possible feed;

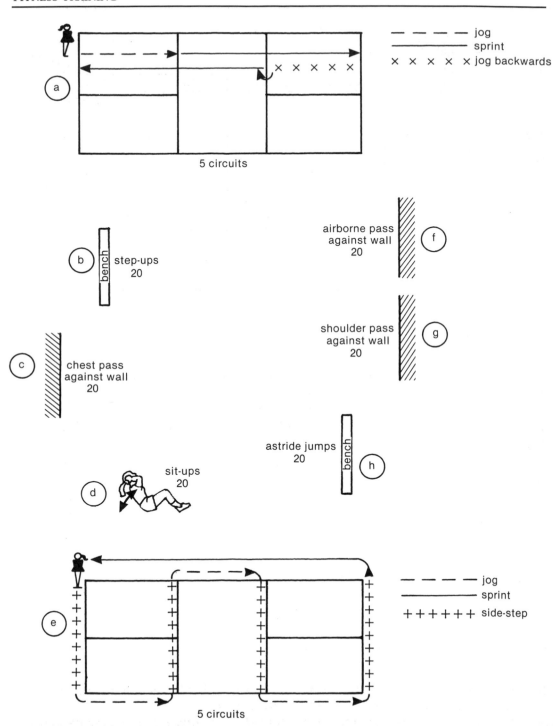

Fig 198 Skill and exercise circuit.

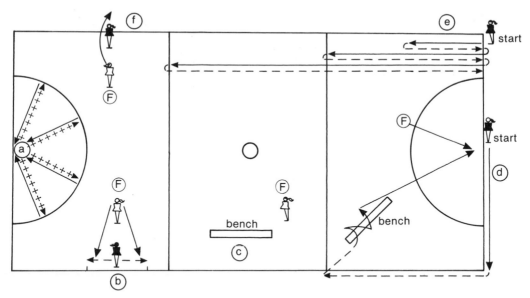

Fig 199   Strength and stamina circuit.

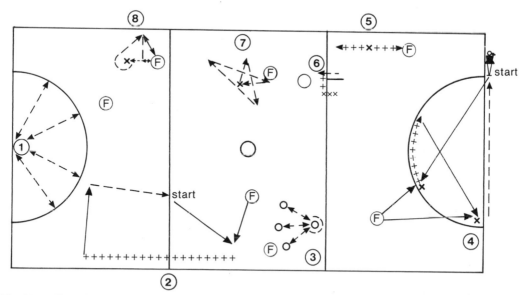

Fig 200   Stamina circuit based on good footwork.

(d) sprint to a mark from the start position, side-step around the front of the circle and sprint to the opposite corner. Jog along the back-line to the start position and repeat. Feeder can feed at the end of the sprints;

(e) side-step forward to reverse hand the ball back to the feeder using your hand

115

which is closest to her. Quickly move away from her to take a high overhead pass using your other hand. Return the ball to the feeder and repeat with your opposite hand and foot towards the feeder;

(f) using a junction between the lines, quickly move your feet forwards, sidewards and backwards over the line. The feeder can feed the forward movement;

(g) from a position facing the feeder, move to the left to receive and return the ball, followed by a movement away to receive a lob and a run forward to receive a drop pass. Return to the start position and repeat;

(h) from a position facing the feeder, quickly roll off and take a pass to the side. Return this to the feeder and at the same time move back into the central area to take a straight pass. Move back to the start and repeat rolling off to the opposite side.

All of these skill activities stand on their own and can be used as individual practices. In a circuit, stamina is highlighted.

Coaches should remember that whatever fitness training they choose to do they must understand why it will make them better. It must be progressive as their fitness improves and above all it must be varied and interesting so that the players do not become bored. Fitness is fun when introduced in an enjoyable manner.

Summary
- To perform efficiently for an hour game, each player must achieve a high fitness level.
- Netball is a game of short bursts and recovery, being more anaerobic than aerobic, but players recover faster if they have good aerobic fitness, which brings the oxygen back to the tired muscles faster. Netball fitness should require the training of both the aerobic and anaerobic energy systems.
- Strength, speed and suppleness are equally important and should be trained within any programme.
- Fitness training can be boring and coaches should explore the many ways of training fitness in order to keep the interest of the players. Training can be with steady runs, fartlek type activities, interval running, shuttle runs or activity or skill circuits.
- All players should be trained to monitor their own pulse rate.
- Coaches should plan a training schedule for all-year-round fitness.

8 Coaching

What makes someone a coach? This is a very difficult question to answer as there is no standard role model of a successful coach. All coaches are different. Their coaching will be affected by their own personality and also by the nature of the group they are working with. They will, however, have one thing in common and that is a wish to help players to get the best out of themselves – to achieve their potential. Coaches will need to fulfil the role of:

(i)   a teacher – with the ability to communicate and pass on knowledge;
(ii) a trainer – with the knowledge and ability to train the body to cope with the physical demands of the game;
(iii) a leader – setting standards of behaviour and dress both on and off the court;
(iv) a friend – with the ability to listen, be sympathetic, trustworthy and yet remain totally fair.

Fulfilling these roles is not an easy task and that is why coaches are in such demand. In this book I have tried to provide some of the knowledge which all coaches need. Transmitting this knowledge to players requires the coach to call upon a wide range of skills and abilities. I would like to end by passing on a few hints and tips which I have picked up during my many years of coaching and I hope that they will prove helpful to any budding coach. Do not be put off by the wide demands of the role, you will find that helping young players to do well is a very rewarding way of spending your leisure time.

HINTS AND TIPS

Planning and Organization

1. Set yourself aims or goals:

(a) long-term goals for a season. These will vary depending on the age and ability of your group, the length of time you have with them and their competitive commitments for the season;
(b Short-term goals. Make a note of the skills and knowledge which the players will need to acquire during the season in order to achieve your long-term goal. Break down these skills and put them in some sort of order to fit them into your session plans throughout the season. Give yourself a number of short term goals which you will hope to achieve as the season progresses.

2. Plan your training:

(a) decide where you are going to train;
(b) decide how long it will last;
(c) decide whether it will be indoors or outdoors.

3. Plan your needs:

(a) decide what equipment you need;
(b) decide who is going to be responsible

for bringing the equipment to the session;
(c) decide if you need an umpire.

4. Plan your practices:

(a) decide which practices you will use;
(b) decide the order;
(c) decide how many players you will be working with;
(d) decide where you will practise, remembering that safety must figure high in your planning.

5. Plan your sessions:

(a) this depends on how imminent your next match or tournament is;
(b) decide what the content of your session will be. A standard pattern for your training sessions could be as shown in the list below, but you need to vary this pattern from time to time according to the needs of your squad. Always remember that the warm-up and cool-down are essential and should not be missed out.

| Warm-up | usually some form of running activity |
| Stretching | exercises to prepare the body for action |

Skill Training

Conditioned game	see page 120
Competitive game	
Cool-down	jogging and stretching aimed to bring the body back to normal temperature

6. Plan for safety:

(a) remember the players are in your hands;

(b) be aware of any possible hazards and remove them before you start;
(c) have a first aid box handy and organize someone to be responsible for it.

Remember that early planning is essential in order to make everything run smoothly. It is also worth taking some time to prepare the training beforehand, so that your job is easier at the actual session.

Communication

All the planning, organization and knowledge in the world will be to little avail if you are unable to pass this information on to the players. This requires the skill of communication; here are a few tips:

(i) be seen – stand where all the players can see you easily. This can vary but normally it is in a position at the side where you can see all of them. Avoid standing in the middle or in a position where there are players behind you.
(ii) be heard – use your voice wisely; be clear, use short explanations and only give input when it is necessary, making sure it is vital and meaningful. Be aware of the acoustics of the facility in which you are working. Only gather the groups around you if you are unable to be heard. Learn to use your voice to easily start and stop your groups. If you have difficulty in stopping them, use a whistle, but make sure that they are aware that the whistle means stop;
(iii) use demonstrations to illustrate what you are looking for – there are many ways of doing this, but however you choose to get your message across try to keep it clear and simple. Decide who is going to give the demonstration and how, making sure everyone can see and

hear what is going on. Use yourself with slow motion movements to direct their attention to the specific points which you wish to put over; use a player whom you have noticed is doing exactly what you are looking for; use a player or group of players, whom you have trained, to demonstrate a particular point, practice or tactical manoeuvre. Do not be frightened to show skills at a slow speed to emphasize points but always follow up by showing them at the correct speed so that the players can get the feeling of the whole movement.

(iv) use visual aids if you find that they are an aid to your communication – use magnetic boards to illustrate moves and positioning; use chalk and a board; use useful feedback material which you have gathered from earlier match play; use video replays if you have the facilities to do this. Remember that these are only aids to communication and should only be used when and if you feel that they can add to or support the coaching points that you are wishing to get over. I have never been a coach who sits players down in front of a television screen unless I have given them specific guidelines or certain points to look for. I do, however, find video recordings of matches very useful for my own viewing in order to pick out what went well or individual difficulties which I can try to put right in the following coaching sessions.

Observation

This is one of the most difficult but essential skills a coach needs to acquire. It is an ability to see what is happening and then to be able to respond accordingly. In order to do this the coach must be very knowledgeable about what is correct and must be able to carry around with her a mental picture of the ideal technique for all the skills of the game. This requires knowledge which can be obtained from books, coaching materials and coaching videos. It also requires time spent watching players during matches and training sessions to learn these observation skills. Here are a few tips:

(i) watch players who are successful and try to spot why they are achieving success. Is it because they are more skilful than their opponent, quicker or because their timing is better?

(ii) watch matches. Try to find out why one team is more successful than the other, who the strong players are, who the weak players are, which moves are going well, what is going badly, how, where and when possession is lost and what could be done to improve the situation.

Make notes to help you with further planning. What you see will give you the material for your next training session. You are learning to make an evaluation on what you see and you will begin to fall into the pattern of planning – practice – observation – evaluation – planning;

(iii) watch other coaches working. See whether the players are responding to the coach, if they are doing what has been asked and if the players are successful. Try to see why they are being successful or unsuccessful. Refer to that mental picture and try to spot whether they are correct or incorrect. Decide if it is because of their footwork or the lack of a follow through. Observe how the coach gives information, if she is in good contact with her group and how she is achieving this. Use any opportunity to train and develop your own observation skill as this can be the key to your success as a coach.

Working with Groups

Any coach must develop her skills when working with groups of players. Most of the coaching will be done with a group containing players who can differ widely in their abilities. The coach will have to make many decisions:

(i) whether to have smaller groups either of mixed ability or of equal ability. There are advantages in both methods;
(ii) how to organize and place the groups on the court. Safety must be taken into account. Use line markings on the court to help you to indicate areas for each group. Good spacing will make it easier for you to observe what each group is doing;
(iii) when to move a practice on. Try to move on as soon as the technique has been mastered. If this takes longer than you think, change the practice but stay with the technique. Staying with the same practice for too long can lead to frustration and boredom and the aims of the practice will be lost.

Coaching within the Practice Game

In my experience this is the part of coaching which is the most difficult but it is the most vital part as it is the time when you are able to see whether the group and the individual coaching which you have done is successful:

(i) learn to use your voice sparingly but when you do, make your contribution short and sharp – be confident;
(ii) learn to watch the one specific coaching point and ignore others. Make sure your players are aware of the particular skill that you are observing.

The common fault is to be carried away by other things that are happening – stick to the point;
(iii) if a skill breaks down be prepared to stop the game and discuss with the players the reason why the breakdown has occurred. Try to correct it by repeating the move successfully.
(iv) if the skill that you are coaching is successful be prepared to give praise. Even consider trying to repeat the successful movement in order to let the players get the feeling of success.
(v) make the players use the skill or tactic which you have coached within the game by setting your own rules or conditions on the game. This is called 'conditioning the game'. If you have coached the use of the underarm pass make all passes into the circle underarm. If toss-ups have already been coached, restart the game when the ball has gone out of court by a toss-up instead of a throw-in. In this way more players will have the experience of being involved in a toss-up situation on the court. If throwing techniques have already been coached and you wish all players to step into the throw, then do not allow the throw to be defended. If shooting from close to the post has already been coached, limit the shooting to a marked area close to the post.

Coaching during a Match (Fig 201)

The rules of netball do not allow coaching during match play. Any coaching input from the coach to the players must therefore be made during the intervals. This skill should improve with a coach's experience. Her feedback to the players will be based on her observation and her evaluation of what is happening. Her observation can be helped by:

Fig 201 The author talks to the England captain during the interval.

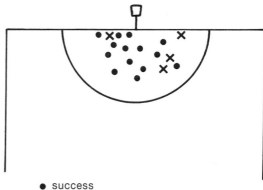

● success
✗ failure

Fig 202 Shooting accuracy.

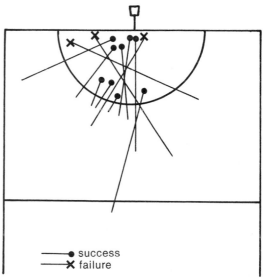

——● success
——✗ failure

Fig 203 Wing attack feeding.

(i) keeping short notes during the play;
(ii) using the substitutes to monitor specific points, possibly points or areas of play which you have been emphasizing in your coaching session. For example: the success rate of the centre pass; where the shots are being taken from (*see* Fig 202); where the wing attack is feeding the circle from (*see* Fig 203); and the interceptions or deflections being made by the wing defence.

Whatever information you wish to pass on to the players it must be constructive, positive and concise. Above all remember to give praise and to keep up the morale of the squad whether they are winning or losing. One player you may need to calm down and steady whilst another you may need to encourage and boost. Whatever the score, always find some area where they have achieved success. Try to remain calm, controlled and supportive whatever the state of the match.

Natural Progression of Practices

I have always found it useful to plot my practices using the following guidance chart. This chart should help the coach who is just starting out to plan her practice at the correct level rather than beginning with a practice which is too difficult. She needs to remember that in order to

121

(i)   **Speed of practice;** perform   – standing still,
                                          – walking pace,
                                          – jogging pace,
                                          – full pace.

(ii) **Begin without the ball and then with the ball**

(iii) **Throwing activities;** perform – standing still to standing still,
                                         – standing still to moving target,
                                         – moving to standing still target,
                                         – moving to moving target.

(iv) **Numbers;** work individually, in pairs and then fours,
                    work individually, in threes and then sixes.
      This makes organization within coaching sessions much easier as pairs to threes
      causes difficulties.

(v)   **Use of defenders;** perform practices – without defenders,
      See Examples given below   – with shadow defenders,
                                                 – with full defending,
                                                 – with more than full defending.

(vi) **Use practised skills in a conditioned game.**

Fig 204   A guidance chart.

improve, a player must achieve success and therefore simple progressions are important – how often are children asked to run down the court passing a ball to one another – a highly difficult practice? You may find the Guidance Chart (*Fig 204*) useful when planning practices.

Examples of the use of Defenders

Practice for a shooter learning to pass out of the circle in order to receive the ball back closer to the post:

(i)   work without defenders using two feeders positioned on the circle edge;
(ii) work with defender aiming to be a body for the shooter to move around;
(iii) work with a defender working to stop the shooter;
(iv) put two or even three defenders in the circle so that the shooter has to work very hard to achieve success. This is often called a pressure practice as the player is having to work even harder than she would have to do in a match situation.

Practices, Formations and Numbers

It is useful to have handy patterns and formations for practices so that whatever number of players you are working with you can visualize a practice using that number of players. Again, I have always found the following chart a useful guide – after a while it all becomes very easy.

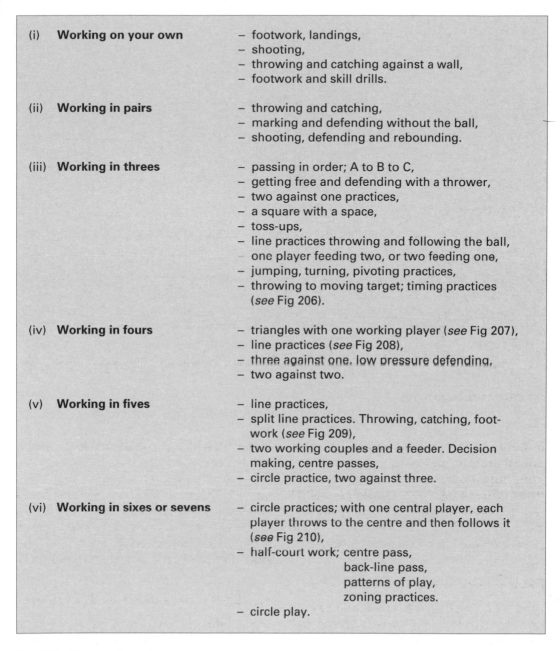

(i)	**Working on your own**	– footwork, landings, – shooting, – throwing and catching against a wall, – footwork and skill drills.
(ii)	**Working in pairs**	– throwing and catching, – marking and defending without the ball, – shooting, defending and rebounding.
(iii)	**Working in threes**	– passing in order; A to B to C, – getting free and defending with a thrower, – two against one practices, – a square with a space, – toss-ups, – line practices throwing and following the ball, – one player feeding two, or two feeding one, – jumping, turning, pivoting practices, – throwing to moving target; timing practices (*see* Fig 206).
(iv)	**Working in fours**	– triangles with one working player (*see* Fig 207), – line practices (*see* Fig 208), – three against one, low pressure defending, – two against two.
(v)	**Working in fives**	– line practices, – split line practices. Throwing, catching, footwork (*see* Fig 209), – two working couples and a feeder. Decision making, centre passes, – circle practice, two against three.

(vi)	**Working in sixes or sevens**	– circle practices; with one central player, each player throws to the centre and then follows it (*see* Fig 210),
		– half-court work; centre pass,
		                     back-line pass,
		                     patterns of play,
		                     zoning practices.
		– circle play.

Fig 205   Types of practice.

All of these hints and tips will be of little use unless you are able to motivate players. You must have the ability to communicate enthusiasm, energy and enjoyment. It is your love of the game and the energy which you impart that

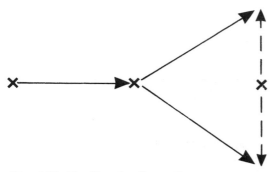

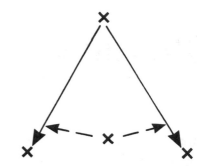

Figs 206–10   Practice formations.

Fig 207.

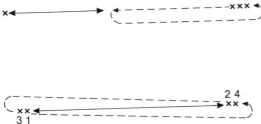

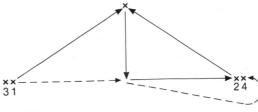

Fig 209.

Fig 208.

Fig 210.

will capture the imagination of the young player and inspire her to get the best out of her own performance and to contribute towards the success of the whole team.

Summary
- Coaching is very demanding but also very rewarding.
- Coaches need to be able to plan and organize, to observe and evaluate performance and to communicate with players.
- Coaches need to be able to work with individuals, groups of players and teams.
- The success of a coach is not only measured by successful results but by the enjoyment of the training sessions by the players and the progress which they make.

Glossary

AENA All England Netball Association, the governing body of netball in England.

Airborne throw A throw which is caught with the feet off the ground and released before the feet are regrounded.

Attacking team The team with possession of the ball.

Back-line The boundary lines at each end of the court

Back-line throw-in A throw-in taken from behind the back-line of the court.

Banding A simple means of dividing the court area into strips across the court.

Bending Moving by taking a curving pathway.

Cardiovascular Concerning the heart and the blood vessels.

Centre circle The small circle in the centre of the court which marks the area from which play starts and restarts after a goal has been scored.

Centre court The middle third of the court.

Centre pass The first pass taken to start or restart the game after a goal is scored.

Circuits A method of exercising where the players move from one exercise to another to complete a circle of activities.

Clearing A move by a player to clear space for another player to move into.

Court linkage A simple system of passing the ball down the court making the best use of space and players.

Cues Signs between players which help to make decisions as to when and where to pass and when and where to move.

Dead-ball situations Times in the game when play is stopped for some reason and is beginning again from a static situation such as a throw-in, a centre pass, a free pass.

Defending
First stage – preventing the opponent from receiving a pass by intercepting. Second stage – defending a player in possession of the ball by covering the intended flight of the ball with the hands or attempting to intercept from a distance of not less than 0.9m (3ft) in front of the thrower.
Third stage – defending a player without the ball by facing her and preventing her from moving in the direction that she wishes.

Defending team The team without possession of the ball.

Dodging any method of getting away from an opponent.

Double marking Two opponents defend one player in order to prevent her from receiving the ball.

Dummy run A movement made by a player into a space which suggests that she is about to receive a pass. She is, however, only creating space for another member of her team to receive the ball.

Endurance running Running which is continuous for at least thirty minutes.

Fartlek runs Endurance runs broken up

by different activities, for example, hopping, striding, short sprints.

Feed   An accurate pass into the shooting circle.

Feint pass   A pretend pass in one direction before releasing in another.

Footwork rule   Limits the movement of the player in possession of the ball.

Free pass   A pass awarded to the non-offending team for any infringement of a rule except obstruction and contact.

Goal-circle   The semi-circle marking the shooting area at each end of the court.

Governing body   The organization responsible for the administration of the game throughout a country.

Holding position   The balanced position achieved by the player in possession of the ball as she makes decisions as to where and how she will pass the ball.

IFNA   International Federation of Netball Association, the controlling body for international competition.

Inter-county tournament   The tournament run annually to decide who will become county champions for that year.

Interval runs   Training runs of various length including rest periods.

Lactic acid   a waste product of exercise which can build up in a muscle causing pain and cramp.

Lunging   Making a long stride with one leg whilst keeping the other leg still.

Man-to-man   A defending method where each player marks her own opponent.

Marking   Staying close to an opponent in order to prevent her from receiving a pass.

Penalty pass   An award made to the non-offending team for any infringement of the obstruction or contact rule. The offending player must stand by the side of the player taking the pass and must

not move until after the ball has been released.

Penalty shot   As above but if the infringement takes place within the shooting circle a shooter may either shoot or pass.

Pivoting   Footwork when the grounded foot is turned without losing contact with the ground.

Rebounding   Jumping to retrieve the ball after a missed shot at goal.

Repositioning   Moving to take up another position after having released the ball.

Reverse handing   Using the hand furthest away from the opponent to reach across turning the hand towards the ball to make a deflection.

Reverse pivot   Changing direction by pivoting on the nearer foot to an opponent, turning away from her and making a move in a different direction.

Rolling off   Getting free by bending away from your opponent, quickly turning your back and moving in a different direction.

Shooting circle   The goal-circle where the GS and GA can attempt to score goals.

Shuttle-runs   Training runs between two points.

Throw-in   Used to return the ball back into play when it has gone out of court.

Toss-up   Used to put the ball back into play when the umpire is unable to make a decision.

Trajectory   The line of flight of the ball as it travels towards its target.

Transverse lines   The two lines across the court dividing it into thirds.

World Championship   An international event held every four years to decide the netball champions of the world.

Zone defence   A method of defending where players work together to cover an area of court and try to intercept the ball as it passes through that area.

Index